BEHAVIORAL SCIENCE IN MANAGEMENT

SAUL W. GELLERMAN

PENGUIN BOOKS

Penguin Books Ltd, Harmondsworth, Middlesex, England
Penguin Books Inc., 7110 Ambassador Road, Baltimore, Maryland 21207, U.S.A.
Penguin Books Australia Ltd, Ringwood, Victoria, Australia
Penguin Books Canada Ltd, 41 Steelcase Road West, Markham, Ontario, Canada
Penguin Books (N.Z.) Ltd, 182–190 Wairau Road, Auckland 10, New Zealand

—

First published 1974

—

Copyright © Saul W. Gellerman, 1974

—

Printed in the United States of America
Set in Monotype Times

Contents

Preface

THE quality of life at work, the quality of work itself, the cost of living and the viability of our economic institutions are all strongly influenced by the way that large organizations are managed. In this book I have tried, in a concise and non-technical manner, to examine how the behavioral sciences have been employed by a few progressive companies in an effort to use their human resources more effectively.

Most of the cases discussed here are North American, simply because they fall within my particular area of experience. However, the book itself has been prepared primarily for European and other non-American readers, who have shown considerable interest in business developments in the United States and Canada which are directly related to productivity and labor costs.

The specific themes that I have chosen to discuss represent major interventions by behavioral scientists in the management process. They are the identification of managerial talent; the attempt to control long-range labor costs through measuring and alleviating employee grievances; the attempt to influence the quality of experience that is generated by doing work; and the attempt to teach those who must collaborate to make a more useful contribution.

At the end of the book, I have selected and edited some further material from other writers that both supplements and illuminates the main text. Each study is relevant to an individual chapter, and can be referred to, if necessary, without interrupting the basic argument.

Behavioral scientists and their managerial allies are attempting nothing less than a deliberate modification of organizational cultures, so as to make them more congenial to the human spirit as we have come to understand it. There are a variety of motives for this effort, but the one that gives it the greatest urgency is the necessity to structure organizations in which ordinary human beings can work willingly and effectively without becoming so frustrated and alienated that they are, in effect, motivated to price themselves and their companies out of the market. This is an ambitious undertaking that is fraught with difficulty, and far from minimizing these difficulties I have sought to highlight them.

The questions raised here may in the foreseeable future become questions of public policy, in which case an informed electorate will be vital to the intelligent resolution of issues involving how and why large organizations are managed. If this book serves at least as an introduction to that process, it will have fulfilled my expectations.

Hohokus, New Jersey   S. W. G.
November 1973

CHAPTER 1

Introduction: What Are the Behavioral Sciences?

MODERN personnel administration has evolved from what was essentially a simplified accounting procedure to the application of several academic disciplines to organizational problems. Among these disciplines are actuarial statistics (which are applied to pension planning), industrial engineering (which is applied to job evaluation and therefore to wage planning) and a group of disciplines known collectively as the 'behavioral sciences'.

This term has come into fashion in recent years to connote the attempt to apply the classical scientific method to the study of human behavior, usually (but not always) through the joint use of methods derived from such disciplines as psychology, sociology, anthropology, or economics. The term 'behavioral science' has no scientific definition of its own; it is a bit of current jargon and for that reason has taken on various implications, some of which are useful for an examination of personnel administration and some of which are not, and none of which in any case is in any way 'official'. For example, the term is frequently understood as applying more to managerial and organizational matters than to broader social or clinical concerns, which is an illogical, but for our purposes quite helpful, narrowing of focus. On the other hand, to some laymen the 'behavioral sciences' are synonymous with their most recent and dramatic products (sensitivity training and its variants) which for our purposes is too restrictive.

Our purposes are to show the effects upon personnel administration in the United States of recent developments in the behavioral sciences (using that term broadly to connote any rigorous, experimental or evidence-based studies of behavior in work settings), and to analyze in some depth a few of the more significant applications of such studies. The United States is chosen as the principal focus of this essay because that is where I have had the bulk of my experience and not because American work in this field has necessarily been more fruitful or relevant than work in Europe or elsewhere. On the contrary, some excellent studies have been reported from Norway, Holland, Sweden, and the United Kingdom to name a few; but it is probably fair to say that until now more – and more varied – work of this kind has been done in the United States than elsewhere. The reader is the best judge of the extent to which the American experience reported here is relevant to his own country. For my part I will only observe that such international consulting experience as I have had has left me far more impressed with the similarity between organizational problems and solutions in various countries than with the differences; granted that there are differences and that they are frequently important.

HOW SCIENTIFIC IS IT?

To some managers, especially those who were trained in engineering or the physical sciences, the term 'behavioral sciences' is affected, pretentious or even self-contradictory. To them, human behavior too often seems capricious; and how can one be 'scientific' about it in any meaningful sense anyway? If the criterion of being scientific is the degree of rigor available to, say, chemistry, the behavioral scientist would ruefully acknowledge that he cannot, alas, be *that* scientific; and perhaps he had better consult the phrase-makers for a more apt job title. Human behavior is the end result of a multiplicity of influences, many of which are hard to identify, let alone measure or control for experimental purposes. The behavioral scientist must always content himself with a greater degree of approximation and unexplained variance than any self-respecting chemist would tolerate. Still, he can take comfort in the fact that his studies are as scientific as his elusive subject matter lets them be, and more importantly, in the knowledge that the question of whether he is scientific at all is pedantic and irrelevant.

That is because the manager seeking guidance on how to

influence behavior in ways that are consistent with the organization's purposes (which is, after all, his job) does not face a choice between the physical and behavioral sciences. There is nothing in physics or chemistry or any of the 'hard' or 'exact' sciences that applies to this problem. His real choice is between the behavioral sciences, such as they are, and *no science at all* – between the behavioral sciences and the accumulated folklore, mythology and superstition that too often passes for traditional managerial wisdom. Given his choice, the behavioral scientist clearly need not apologize for the state of his science (except, perhaps, to his colleagues), and he can point with some pride to significant advances in managerial technique which have flowed directly from his studies.

INFLUENCE OR MANIPULATION?

Before leaving this matter of definitions (which I find tedious) there is one other pseudo-question which, because it arises frequently, must be disposed of. It is whether 'influencing behavior in ways that are consistent with the organization's purposes' is not a euphemism for manipulation. To answer this we must define manipulation. If it is sinister enough to be criticized, 'manipulation' would presumably imply ways of somehow making men act contrary to their own interests, perhaps without their even knowing it. If that is what manipulation is, then it is science fiction and not behavioral science.

Granted that there are fools and that there are people who are clever and unscrupulous enough to exploit them; then nothing that the behavioral sciences has revealed has made such exploitation any easier. Stories of hypnotism, brainwashing and subliminal perception notwithstanding, no one has ever discovered a feasible system for taking command of sensible minds. Mass hysteria occurs, but it is seldom if ever deliberately contrived. Our best defense against manipulation lies in human nature itself, which is usually reflective and skeptical enough to resist (and retaliate effectively against) attempts to use it for anyone else's advantage.

11

Further, the concern with manipulation implies that the purposes of the organization must somehow be inconsistent with those of men in general. But such an inconsistency could not endure for long. Either the organization adapts to the needs of men or it is eventually destroyed; that is what a revolution is. More commonly, organizations adapt themselves to human needs (to cite two current American examples: hiring people previously considered 'unemployable' and investing in methods of curbing environmental pollution). Indeed the real (as opposed to the fantasied) role of the behavioral sciences has been to help organizations adapt their policies and methods to the realities of human nature; to present evidence on how to increase human satisfaction; since ultimately that is less costly than, willingly or otherwise, causing dissatisfaction. In effect, behavioral scientists are busily helping organizations make productivity more of a triumphant personal experience and less of a humiliation or a bore; not out of charity but out of hard practicality since triumphant men are ultimately more productive than defeated men.

Yet with all this effort devoted to enhancing the human spirit, one can legitimately ask who is manipulating whom? In a very real sense, the members of an organization bend it to their needs rather than vice versa; and it has been the role of the behavioral sciences to make this reality both clear and useful to the men who manage organizations. Thus the 'manipulation' issue turns out, upon examination, to lack substance.

IMPACT ON MANAGEMENT

(1) Personnel Selection

The impact of the behavioral sciences upon American personnel management can be traced through three historical stages. Each successive stage broadened, rather than replaced, the previous one and the current scene is essentially an amalgam of all three. The first stage dates from the period after the First World War and was marked by an emphasis on *personnel selection*. This was stimulated by the success of the United States Army in classifying large numbers of draftees and recruits into various occupational specialties by means of intelligence tests. The technology, which was then relatively new, dovetailed neatly with the then recent advent of 'scientific management' and its belief that one could define the 'one best way' in which any job should be done. It seemed to make sense that there would be certain individuals who were more likely, by reason of their inherent abilities or acquired traits, to learn that one best way and then adhere to it faithfully.

The idea that men should be placed in jobs to which their talents and inclinations were fitted, and that those qualities could be reliably (indeed, scientifically) determined, was revolutionary in its day. An enormous number of tests were developed and put to use, in both cases with widely varying sophistication and success; and at their best, very good results were obtained. To the general intelligence-tests were added tests of specific aptitudes and later of occupational interests, and still later tests which attempted to measure or infer personality characteristics. Still later the 'paper-and-pencil' mode of testing was broadened to include situational exercises and patterned interviews.

Largely because of its age, research on personnel selection has been far more extensive and sophisticated than on any other application of behavioral science. Indeed, we know more about how to select people for work than we customarily put to use, and this is one reason why at least some of the controversies and scandals that have developed about the use of tests in recent years (regarding racial discrimination and invasion of privacy) have, alas, been deserved. But rather than dwell on failure to use what we know, we shall use part of this brief essay to review some of the more impressive and recent American advances in the arts of selection. In Chapter 2 we will consider the 'Early Identification of Management Potential' program in the Exxon Corporation. At the end of the book I have included a paper originally written for internal use in Esso Europe, Inc., by a psychologist who was one of the principal architects of this program. It describes the experiences which Esso affiliates in

Europe have had in adapting for their own use a testing procedure that was originally developed in the United States.

(2) Managerial Benevolence

The second stage of behavioral science impact upon personnel administration dates from the mid 1930s and was characterized by an emphasis on fostering employee contentment through various forms of *managerial benevolence*. The theory was that even when men were placed in jobs for which they were fitted, the everyday realities of work were filled with various irritants which, unless they were screened or cancelled out by pleasant experiences, could fester into hostile attitudes and costly behavior such as work restriction or strikes.

In many European countries, the use of various forms of managerial benevolence toward employees developed earlier, and is relied upon more heavily today, than in the United States. With the exception of employee-attitude surveys and supervisory training, most forms of benevolence are more highly developed in Europe than in America, and this condition is likely to continue due to the greater mobility of the American labor force and the consequent traditional emphasis on wages rather than 'benefits' in American payment systems. Despite this difference in emphasis, managerial benevolence played a very important role in American personnel administration during the 1930s and 1940s, and continues to receive significant if diminished attention.

Two events helped to provide the setting for this period in the United States: the first was the publication of the Hawthorne studies which seemed to offer convincing proof that employees were more productive when their needs for attention, respect and acceptance were satisfied, than when they were treated impersonally. Today such a view is regarded as both self-evident and somewhat oversimplified; at the time it was a revelation and a breakthrough. The second event was the approval by the United States Congress of the National Labor Relations Act (1934) which for the first time made the formation of labor unions for the purpose of collective bargaining with employers a legal right.

Thus employers had two more or less simultaneous reasons for interest in learning the arts of benevolence. It seemed both profitable to do it and costly not to do it.

Benevolence in American personnel administration has taken many forms. Some are essentially diversions, such as company-sponsored parties, dinners and athletic teams. Some are essentially assurances of financial security, such as pensions, life insurance, hospitalization and medical insurance and various savings plans. Some are essentially attempts to ensure just and humane treatment, such as supervisory training programs and 'grievance channels' which provide a protected right of appeal when supervisory decisions seem unfair to the employee. Some are essentially searches for remediable sources of dissatisfaction, such as employee-attitude surveys.

Collectively these various efforts to keep people happy have probably done more to maintain faith in the free enterprise system on the part of employees than any other action of American management. Evidently rebellion (of both the political and on-the-job varieties) is more likely to occur under a persistently coercive form of management than one which attempts to demonstrate its concern for the dignity of the individual and the satisfaction of his needs. It is an article of faith among many American personnel managers that the diligent application of benevolent procedures is their best guarantee that workers will not resort to labor unions. Under the American system, unions obtain bargaining rights for employees only when management consents to it or when a majority of employees vote in a government-supervised election to be represented by the union. Managements of American companies whose employees are not represented by unions usually prefer to preserve that situation for the sake of greater flexibility and less exposure to work stoppage. Apart from these benefits, it is difficult to demonstrate any lasting, significant effect of benevolence upon employee behavior. It seems fair to say that the importance of benevolence lies more in what it prevents than in what it produces.

What it produces is sometimes a certain complacency which critics have railed against, at times justifiably. Labor union advocates have called it the 'contented cow' approach, designed to blind the employee to the (presumed) inherent conflict of interest between himself and his employers and therefore to his need for the services of a union as well. Social critics have referred disparagingly to the benevolence approach as the 'cult of the happiness boys'. More to the point, personnel managers have increasingly recognized that, while the benevolence approach is and should be a permanent part of their repertoires, it is not in itself a sufficient answer to the problems of effective manpower utilization. In Chapter 3 we will review some of the more sophisticated applications of this approach which involve the use of employee-attitude studies to monitor the effects of management policies, and which anticipate long-term behavior changes and develop alternative procedures for accomplishing managerial goals without producing undesired behavioral side-effects.

However, this method is not without its difficulties, chief of which is managerial resistance to taking the kinds of action which attitude studies may indicate. In Case Study 2 we will present a paper by one of the leading American experts on attitude studies, in which some of the reasons for this kind of resistance are discussed.

(3) Experimental Intervention

The third stage of behavioral-science impact upon personnel administration dates from the 1960s and is marked by *experimental interventions* to alter job design and organization structure, on the one hand, and the relationships between individuals and between groups, on the other. The experimental approach has been heavily influenced by the job enrichment technique, which will be reviewed in Chapter 4, and by the 'organization development' movement, which will be reviewed in Chapter 5. Case Studies 3 and 4 are papers dealing with job enrichment: first, the notes of a British manager who successfully introduced this method into his department in a refinery; next, the observations of two American consultants on some of the difficulties that are encountered when job enrichment is introduced. And Case Study

5 is an explanation of team building, an organization development technique, by one of its leading American practitioners. The concluding chapter will offer some general observations and some thoughts about the probable future effects of behavioral science on American personnel administration.

. . . AND THE FUTURE

One final introductory point: while I will stress the effects which behavioral science has had upon personnel administration in the United States, it would not be fair to say that these effects have been pervasive or even necessarily dominant. Many American firms are still managed with scant regard, or no more than lip-service, to the implications of the behavioral sciences.

I have deliberately chosen to include papers which emphasize the difficulties of applying the behavioral sciences, so as to avoid giving the wholly unrealistic impression that we have developed sweeping solutions that lend themselves to simple, painless application.

But there are a number of reasons for forecasting that the influence of the behavioral sciences, which is already substantial, will be felt even more heavily in the future. Chief among these are: the fact that many prestigious, opinion-shaping firms have drawn heavily from the behavioral sciences; the publicizing of behavioral research results in management journals and increased emphasis on behavioral science in management development programs; the changing mix of both jobs (more professional and service jobs, fewer unskilled and production jobs) and employees (more highly educated, mobile, relatively affluent employees, fewer low-skilled, passive, economically dependent employees); and the coming of age of the first generation of American managers to have been professionally trained for management. These men are now rising to senior executive levels in many companies. Taken together, these trends indicate that American management is likely to rely upon behavioral research and its applications more heavily than ever. It need hardly be added that similar trends are at work in most European countries, for which reason developments in America may be regarded as at least instructive trends, if not precursors, of what the future may hold for European management

CHAPTER 2

The Search for Tomorrow's Management

DEVELOPING managers in the numbers, quality and depth required to run a major corporation is a time-consuming business. It may take years, even decades, to equip a man with the depth and breadth of comprehension that top management requires. But it is also to a company's advantage to have its executives arrive in positions of command while they are still young enough to handle their jobs with vigor and some prospects of longevity. Simple arithmetic leads, then, to the toughest paradox in management development: if a man's potentialities for top management have not been recognized by the time he is, say, thirty-five years old, it may already be too late to begin trying to qualify him for that level.

Hence the need for some kind of 'early identification' device, through which young men whose potential (if any) for senior managerial responsibilities is just emerging can somehow be singled out from their peers. The problem is not new, but it has been notoriously intractable. Study after study indicated the apparent futility of attempting to predict at long range the way in which managerial careers would evolve. Part of the difficulty lay in the inherent limitations of tests and interviews, but a more serious handicap was the exasperating problem of the criterion: how can you tell whether a test is able to predict executive success when you have no reliable way to measure 'success' itself?

THE EIMP PROGRAM

Despite these obstacles, some long strides forward have been made; and one of the most notable of these has been taken by Exxon Company, USA, a division of Exxon Corporation and its principal operating arm in the United States. (Until recently, these organizations were known as Humble Oil and Refining Company and Standard Oil Company [New Jersey], respectively.) It is based on a uniquely derived series of tests and questionnaires which are used as a supplement to managerial observations. The program, originally known as EIMP (for 'early identification of management potential') is designed to identify younger professional employees who are capable of rising to senior executive levels.

Exxon, like most American companies, prefers to base its estimates of a man's potential on what it has seen him do. But trying to read the implications of current performance for future potential is a tricky and often deceptive exercise. This is especially true during the early phases of a man's career. Exxon's psychologists once did a study which demonstrated that it takes about nine years (on average) before management's year-to-year forecasts of how far a man can go stabilize sufficiently for a really reliable 'fix' to be taken on his prospects.

This may at first seem astonishing. Many managers are accustomed to believing that the ability to judge a man's long-range potential is a skill they ought to have to do their jobs properly, and they therefore assume that they do have it. But behavioral research repeatedly indicates that this is folklore rather than demonstrable fact. Managerial judgement, even by otherwise skilled managers, of young men's long-range potential is notoriously unreliable when put to a serious test. For this reason, Humble and other American companies have put sentiment aside and placed their faith in measures which are demonstrably more reliable – such as the EIMP system. In so doing they are acknowledging reality and not any lack of management skill. On the contrary, the successful application of the EIMP system demands managerial expertise of a very high caliber.

Uncertainty about potential tends to linger so long primarily because young men mature at different rates, and therefore reveal their capabilities at more or less unpredictable points in their careers. Humble executives in charge of the EIMP program feel that you don't *really* know what kind of man you've got until he has been fully tested by several jobs, including at least one management job. 'Unfortunately,' they observe, 'by that time a lot of ambitious young men may have become impatient and left you. If they actually were capable of rising to upper-level management jobs, their departure represents a loss we simply cannot afford.'

THE PDS TEST PROGRAM

It was precisely that argument that persuaded a frankly skeptical Humble management to attempt some field trials in 1962 with a specially devised test program known as the 'Personnel Development Series', or PDS, which was based on the EIMP research. Company psychologists suggested that tests like these might enable Humble to identify high management potential sooner, before management judgements were likely to crystallize in a consensus. Actually they had good reason to be confident of their proposal. Six years earlier, Humble's parent company (Jersey Standard) had conducted a massive experimental testing program on some 500 top and middle managers. This study marked the first large-scale demonstration of strong correlations between *certain* test scores and the relative success of managers in a major corporation. That is, those managers who had been rising most rapidly through the hierarchy, and who eventually rose farthest, could be distinguished from those who advanced more slowly by characteristic ways of responding to certain tests. This gave rise to the hope, which the 1962 trial was designed to explore, that those response patterns (or others like them) could be used to predict which young managers would be promoted faster and farther than others.

By 1966, evidence of PDS's effectiveness had become so convincing that its use began to spread to many divisions of the Humble organization. During their first two years of employment, many professional workers (such as geophysicists and engineers) are now invited to take the series on a voluntary basis. At the time of writing, about 4000 men have been tested, which amounts to about one third of Exxon's management and professional group. The program is now geared to test new men regularly. Although Exxon executives retain a certain healthy skepticism toward any indirect means of estimating human potential, they have also acquired a healthy respect for the results obtained by PDS.

THE USES OF PDS

Exxon's prime use of the PDS series is to help in picking young men for tryouts in supervisory jobs. Another application derives from the company's approach to salary planning, which considers both current performance and an estimate of how high a man can rise beyond his present job. The theory is that men who can go all the way to the top need both a hefty reward to keep them from being lured away, and the challenge of an even more affluent future to keep them motivated to earn it. The effect of PDS in the salary system is indirect, but important; it encourages managers to take a searching look at each man's managerial potential.

PDS also serves as a sort of *lingua franca* within the Exxon Company, USA. In any company, when men are transferred across functional lines either to broaden their experience or to relieve personnel imbalances, there is a certain natural reluctance on the part of the receiving group to accept at face value the appraisal of the transferee submitted by the sending group. This phenomenon, which is not at all uncommon in decentralized organizations, results in a sort of inertia which slows management's efforts to 'cross-fertilize' its developing talent. As a result, men who are capable of developing general management skills are sometimes trapped within a single functional line of advancement. However, PDS results mean much the same thing from function to function, and thus provide an acceptable way of relating individual managerial abilities to a common standard.

The tests themselves are administered in two phases: the first for relatively new employees, dealing with abilities that are more or less stable, as well as certain aspects of personal history up to that point, and the second after about five years of employment. It deals with subsequent experiences both on and off the job. All told there are two reasoning tests (verbal and non-verbal), one test of managerial judgement, one attitude questionnaire and two personal history forms. The latter are by far the most potent, interesting and controversial parts of the PDS program.

THE VALUE OF BIOGRAPHICAL RECORDS

The rationale for exploring personal history lies in the behavioral science concept that early behavior tends to persist. Although there are plenty of exceptions, adult behavior trends are usually discernible (in different form, of course) in adolescence or even earlier. Humble has learned that its more successful top managers tend, among other things, to be at home in leadership roles, prepared to take risks, and rather broad-ranging in their interests. More importantly, the origins of these behavior patterns were evidently apparent when these executives were much younger. Therefore, rather than *ask* people whether they have these characteristics (which is the strategy of the conventional 'personality tests', and a fairly obvious reason for their comparative uselessness as predictors of behavior), biographical records like that used by Humble look for actual instances of these traits in the prior activities of the individual. The biographical record is, in effect, a written interview, but in much greater depth and detail than most face-to-face interviews. The results, at least by comparison with other paper-and-pencil techniques, are remarkably predictive.

Managers of PDS confess to a certain uneasiness with that word 'biographical'. 'It suggests,' they say, 'that we are trying to perpetuate some kind of dynasty by bringing into management only people with a particular kind of background. That just isn't true. First of all, that would be a very inefficient way to utilize our available manpower. But if you look at those instruments, you'll see that they are actually built to pick up evidence of the kinds of behavior we're interested in, almost regardless of the kind of environment that the man happened to be in at the time. Rural people, for example, do not express leadership in quite the same ways as city people. These tests actually put examinees on the same starting line, regardless of their origins.'

DOES PDS MEASURE THE RIGHT SKILLS?

Because PDS results are essentially a comparison between any individual's scores and those of a previous successful generation of managers, it is always possible that the tests may be measuring obsolete abilities. Psychologists at Exxon Company, USA, claim they can protect the company against that danger. All of the accumulated PDS data (which by now fill an entire room at Exxon's Houston headquarters) are periodically re-evaluated to determine whether the scoring or the standards need to be changed. So far, some of the questions designed to pick up underlying behavior patterns have been modified, but there has been no need to alter the patterns themselves. Perhaps that is because the chief characteristic of the men who do well on PDS is 'a sort of built-in immunity to obsolescence.' In other words, instead of passively awaiting change, these men anticipate it, adapt to it, and not infrequently become the principal agents of change themselves. Exxon denies that it is looking for a stereotype, but if there is one at all it is evidently of a man too intent on influencing his environment to submit to it; too responsive to his environment to limit his own tactics to any stereotype.

The effect of PDS is to give at least a temporary advantage to men who have already begun to demonstrate the qualities of an effective manager, and to handicap (again, at least temporarily) those who have not yet begun to demonstrate them. Exxon psychologists concede the point, but add frankly, 'This is life. The fact is that if a man has not begun to show some kind of evidence of leadership by the time we test him, the statistical chances that he will begin to show them later are rather small. Obviously, we are interested in the so-called "late bloomer", and that is why we give a second PDS series five years after the first, and why the biographical part of PDS is as lengthy as it is. We want to look for leadership in any aspect of a person's background where it is likely to show up.'

HOW PDS IS APPLIED

At Exxon Company, USA, many new professional employees are now invited to go through PDS. Only a handful have ever declined, despite the fact that Exxon does not disclose the results to examinees. (The company questions the value of such discussions if a qualified professional is not available to interpret the scores, and in view of the volume of testing this is not feasible.) This pattern of early coverage is considered the company's best guarantee that managerial potential will not be overlooked during the early years of employment. Actual testing and scoring is handled by the Employee Relations Department at Exxon Company, USA, but the data are put to use by line management, two organizational levels (not managerial levels) above the immediate superior of the employee. For example, if a geologist in a field exploration unit takes PDS, his results will be sent to the manager of the regional exploration division above the district headquarters to which his immediate supervisor reports. Putting the data midway between the immediate superior and Humble itself is a deliberate ploy to ensure that PDS influences management decisions neither too greatly nor too little.

In practice, periodic development reviews consider both PDS and recent observations of the individual's work. There is no prescribed way of 'weighting' the two, although PDS probably gets more stress during the early years and progressively less as the man's actual record of accomplishments accumulates. When PDS projections of how high the man could rise agree with management's projections, based on observed performance, his potential is considered confirmed (at least for that year). When discrepancies arise, a thorough review of the man's record is undertaken in the hope of resolving them. One Exxon executive has said that if PDS accomplished nothing else than requiring that these reviews be made, it would have paid for itself right there. If the discrepancy remains unresolved, management usually opts for more data by providing a new (lateral) assignment or by continuing the man in his current job.

THE BENEFITS OF PDS

However, the real payoff in PDS is in the number of high-potential men who are successfully identified *before* their promise became apparent to management in the normal course of performance appraisal. This, after all, is the essential purpose of the system. To date, that figure runs at the rate of about 73 per cent of all identified high-potential men with less than four years of service. In effect, then, PDS triples the number of high-potential identifications during the early years of employment. Considering its low operating cost, Exxon clearly regards PDS as a bargain.

However, the benefits of PDS cannot be expressed entirely in statistics. Its contribution to furthering individual careers is at least as important as the company's tables of confirmed high-potential men. One recent series of examples occurred in connection with the industry-wide trend to decrease oil exploration on land in favor of undersea exploration. The trend created a surplus in the job category known as 'land men', that is, men who were responsible for negotiating leases for exploratory drilling. Because US offshore drilling rights are negotiated with a single 'landlord' (the federal government), the displaced men could not be completely absorbed by transferring them to offshore operations. However, a number of these men had very promising PDS results, which made them more than welcome in several other company units despite their previously specialized backgrounds. Exxon Company, USA managers increasingly accept PDS scores as evidence of individual adaptability which makes previous experience almost irrelevant. (Previous *performance*, of course, is very relevant.)

On balance, the advantage of PDS appears to lie mainly in its ability to provide what had not been obtainable by other means: an early, reliable indication of the potential to advance far and fast. As soon as this evidence is confirmed by the management's on-the-scene observations, the high-potential man is moved ahead toward responsibility levels that will both test him and teach him to handle still heavier responsibilities. It is this head start, these extra few years of recognition at a time when recognition is ordinarily much harder to win, that represents the real contribution of PDS to the management development program in Exxon Company, USA.

ITS ADAPTABILITY TO DIFFERENT CULTURES

More recently, Exxon overseas affiliates have investigated the adaptability of the PDS system to its operations outside the United States. The tests were translated into Norwegian, Danish and Dutch and adapted to fit local cultural conditions. They were then administered to large groups of managers in affiliates in Norway, Denmark and Holland and the results were correlated with the relative rate of salary progression of each man, which is an objective if not necessarily entirely pertinent criterion of upward progression through the managerial hierarchy. Comparable results to those obtained in the United States were derived in this European sample, suggesting that whatever it is that makes a manager successful in this international oil company does not differ substantially from country to country. Still more support for the apparent 'universality' of management success factors comes from a similar study completed by affiliates in Latin America.

BEHAVIORAL RESEARCH IN OTHER
SELECTION PROCEDURES

The studies that have been conducted by Exxon affiliates throughout the world represent, in my view, the most sophisticated use of paper-and-pencil tests by any American company. It is worth noting however that other US companies have begun to approach the problem of management selection through other techniques derived from behavioral research. One of these, the 'assessment center' procedures pioneered in the United States by the American Telephone and Telegraph Company, is familiar to many European executives since it is comparable to the officer candidate selection procedures used by military and civil service selection boards. Another, being pioneered by IBM and a handful of other American companies, is based on a sharply focused analysis of certain quite specific aspects of job performance. Through these and other research applications, some of the mystique (and more importantly, some of the vulnerability to extremely costly errors) that has traditionally surrounded managerial selection is gradually being cleared away.

Suggested Reading:

1. CASSENS, F. P., *Cross Cultural Dimensions of Executive Life History Antecedents* (*Biographical Information*). Doctoral dissertation, Louisiana State University, 1966. (Published by The Creativity Research Institute of the Richardson Foundation, Inc., Greensboro, N.C.)

2. LAURENT, H., 'Research on the Identification of Management Potential', in MYERS, J. A., JR (ed.), *Predicting Managerial Success*, Ann Arbor, *Foundation for Research on Human Behavior*, 1968, pp. 1–34.

3. SPARKS, C. P., 'Identify Management Potential Early', *Hydrocarbon Processing*, 1967, pp. 46, 209–11.

4. LAURENT, H., *Cross-Cultural Cross-Validation of Empirically Validated Tests*, Experimental Publication System, American Psychological Association, Washington, D.C., issue no. 2, 1969.

CHAPTER 3

Elegant Solutions to Untidy Problems

AN elegant solution alters the causes of a problem so as to eliminate or better still to prevent it, without causing undesired side-effects. By this standard our 'solutions' to many personnel problems are very inelegant indeed. In fact, one can argue that some of the most excruciating difficulties we have in managing people are the unforeseen, unintended side-effects of 'solutions' to problems which ostensibly had little or nothing to do with people.

In attempting to cope with such side-effects we too often ignore the extraordinary subtlety and sensitivity of most humans to the *totality* of their experience, and seek the cause instead in some narrow, possibly unimportant, but at least familiar corner of their experience. Thus, when employees begin to behave inconveniently (for example, to strike, quit, delay or restrict production) we are too prone to assume that some agitator has upset them or that some of our supervisors have dealt with them clumsily. We are much less likely to seek the cause in some managerial action taken for good sound reasons and having in any case no obvious relationship to the troublesome behavior. And we are perhaps least likely to seek the answer by asking the people whose behavior is troubling us to tell us what is troubling them.

REBIRTH OF THE ATTITUDE SURVEY

We have not, in other words, become nearly as expert as we should or could be in the art of understanding behavior through analyzing people's perceptions of their own situations, which is the essential purpose of the employee-attitude survey. This old-established, frequently ignored and under-utilized management tool is now attracting new attention and sophisticated application in several American firms (notably Texas Instruments and IBM).

THE TIME-LAG EFFECT

Part of the stimulus comes from a recognition of the 'time-lag effect', largely as a result of research by Professor Rensis Likert of the University of Michigan. Although most of the work on which his theories are based was done in the United States, subsequent studies in Europe and elsewhere, notably by Shell Oil, have demonstrated that Likert's ideas are valid on an international scale. The essence of Likert's approach to management problems is that the cumulative effects of employee helpfulness or harassment eventually show up on the profit-and-loss statement in the form of reduced or higher labor costs, and that these forms of behavior become significant chiefly when they have been practised long enough to become habitual. That is to say, habitual sabotage is more destructive than occasional sabotage and habitual precision is more profitable than occasional precision. The key to lower labor costs is therefore to concentrate on habit formation; to encourage helpful habits and to discourage those that harass or impede the productive processes of the organization.

This much is obvious, but it is at this point that Likert's ideas become both subtle and vitally important. Actions are the products of beliefs; people try to act in ways that are consistent with what they believe about their jobs, their employers and their long-range interests, to name a few key factors. But beliefs also have a habitual quality to them: they develop through the gradual accumulation of experience, supported by confirming experiences and the relative absence of contradictory experience. Thus all forms of employee behavior, regardless of whether they are welcome or abhorrent to management, have essentially the same basis in employee beliefs. To them, what they are doing is the right, decent, logical thing to do because their experience has taught them this. (The controlling effects of experience upon behavior are of course not limited to employees. Managers act as they do for essentially the same reasons; the difference lies in the experiences themselves and not in the processes whereby they cumulatively affect beliefs.)

There is thus a certain inertia or momentum to be coped with in trying to influence behavior and, therefore, beliefs. The forces which ultimately determine whether labor costs shall be unprofitably high or competitively low gather strength gradually over months or even years, and consequently the critical factor to be dealt with in any realistic cost-control program is time itself. But while beliefs are the ultimate causes of sustained actions (i.e. a change in beliefs will lead to a change in behavior), they do not change at the same rate. Comparatively speaking, beliefs are more volatile and behavior is more sluggish, although lasting changes in either are seldom quick. This is the 'time-lag': events which may cumulatively reshape beliefs do so slowly because beliefs are based on the totality of experience and not simply on recent experiences. Even after beliefs have begun to change, old behavior patterns will tend to continue for a time: such is the force of habit.

LABOR COST CONTROL

Translating all this theory into practical managerial terms: the variable (and therefore controllable) part of labor costs is usually the result of reactions to events in the relatively remote past. Action taken today to affect attitudes will have effects months or possibly years from now. Today's and even tomorrow's labor costs have already been determined and are no longer controllable. The sophisticated company therefore works on the attitude-behavior-labor cost cycle with a substantial lead time, beginning with a measurement of attitudes and periodically monitoring them to determine the direction they have taken. That direction, if not altered, could very well be a harbinger of the direction which labor costs must inevitably take, and consequently the measurement can serve as a sort of early warning system with regard to costs.

While attitude surveys can measure, in the sense of indicating the frequency distribution for various kinds of beliefs among various subgroups of employees, mere measurement is not sufficient for managerial purposes. The purpose after all is cost control and not an exercise of academic inquisitiveness. Consequently the survey must diagnose as well as measure: it must explain the reasoning that leads to the beliefs that are summarized in the statistical tables, or the experiences on which those beliefs are founded. Only then can action be addressed to causes rather than to symptoms and only then do elegant solutions become possible. Thus subsequent measurements become checks on the effectiveness of the actions taken and not a mere repetition of an exercise. In this manner the attitude survey can become a managerial planning and control procedure of the first importance.

The two case examples which follow are drawn from the recent experience of my consulting firm. While the identity of the client companies obviously cannot be revealed, I will vouch for the fact that the cases are real and, within the limits of available space and concealment of confidential information, faithfully portrayed. These examples are not purported to be representative of attitude survey findings but rather were selected because they illustrate, perhaps more vividly than other cases in our files, certain important principles of *long-range labor cost control*. In using that term I obviously intend to suggest that short-range measures such as manpower reductions or detailed reporting procedures are likely (especially when coercively applied) to create long-range costs far greater than the savings that they generate, and that sustained low labor costs (as distinguished from spasmodic reductions) are more likely to result from the consistent application of long-range methods, including the attitude analysis procedure outlined above.

THE SOLUTION OF AN EXISTING PROBLEM

A technical service organization acquired an enviable reputation for the excellence of its work, and partly for this reason its sales grew very rapidly. There was soon a substantial backlog of unfilled orders, and the technical representatives (TRs) themselves were burdened with a heavy workload and demanding schedules. Attempts to alleviate the problem by hiring additional TRs were only partially effective, since very few trained men were available and the company was therefore obliged to put its newly hired men through a lengthy training procedure. However, these problems were viewed as the price of success and were accepted cheerfully enough until a complication developed which very nearly proved disastrous. This was a sharp increase in the percentage of TRs who resigned in order to accept other employment. It quickly became apparent that if this trend continued, either the work completion schedule would have to be extensively set back, or risks would have to be taken with quality, or both. Either development would have exposed the company to what it considered unacceptably severe competitive threats.

The two most obvious alternatives – to increase the hiring rate or to increase the wage rate – were considered and rejected. Trainees were instructed by experienced TRs, so to hire more trainees would simply divert more of the overburdened TRs from their regular duties and exacerbate the already severe problem in the field. More importantly, the action would at best only compensate for the basic problem: the loss of experienced men. To make the problem at least temporarily worse without contributing to its reduction or elimination would obviously have been a most inelegant solution and it was therefore rejected. Wage rates were already high by industry standards and while instances were known in which TRs had evidently been seduced by extraordinarily high offers, to increase the general wage rate sufficiently to prevent such losses would have raised labor costs to unprofitable levels. Further, such cost increases would in effect have been permanent; there was little likelihood of the company effectively disembarrassing itself of an uneconomical wage structure in the future. Thus wage action sufficient to cope with the problem was neither affordable nor sustainable and would in any case have created a more intractable financial problem than the one it was designed to solve.

The requirements of an elegant solution in this case were that the resignation rate be reduced to tolerable levels without creating undesirable side effects of such severity as to cancel out the gain, and to do this rapidly enough to protect the company's competitive position. The critical need was for an understanding of *why* the resignation rate had increased, since only with such knowledge could effective responses be deliberately fashioned. It did not suffice to know the kind of jobs that the resigned TRs went to (that was their solution and did not necessarily indicate the problem they were trying to solve; for that matter it did not necessarily solve their problem either since several of them eventually re-applied to their original employers). Nor was it sufficient merely to ask them their reasons for leaving, since some are reluctant to be candid, some are candid but unable to articulate their reasons adequately and many, perhaps most, men are aware only of what finally precipitated their decision and not of the experiences that predisposed them to be precipitated. Indeed, the 'precipitators' were usually events which could occur by chance to anyone, such as being irritated by a busy supervisor's brusque remark or noticing an advertisement by a competitor. It was the 'predisposers' that mattered, the events which gradually made the individual susceptible to inevitable annoyances or temptations. If these could be identified, an elegant solution might be achieved.

For these reasons an attitude survey was arranged, beginning with a series of interviews with a small sample of TRs to determine topics of general concern to them, and followed shortly afterward by a questionnaire completed by the entire group. The completed questionnaires were coded for computer analysis and the responses to each question were then tabulated demographically (i.e. displayed separately by subgroup such as younger *v.* older employees, or by location) and correlated with responses to other questions. The latter procedure sought to identify topics which evoked attitudes clearly associated with the expressed attitude toward remaining with or leaving the company, which was itself the topic of a special question. In this manner it was also hoped that predisposing factors might be uncovered.

Several were, and for our purposes the most revealing of these was a negative correlation between the expressed interest in remaining in the company and the degree to which the TRs felt that their education was utilized by their work; that is, those who indicated the greatest interest in leaving tended to be those who felt that their education was least utilized by their work.

In what follows it is important for the reader to bear in mind that this clue and the resulting action were only part of a much larger pattern and that it would grossly oversimplify the facts to suggest that the subsequent events could be accounted for entirely by actions related to this clue; to present the case in its entirety would require more space than we have and more patience than the author (and perhaps the reader) have to offer.

In any case, the clue recalled comments by TRs in interviews that the job specialization system resulted eventually in a certain repetitiveness and loss of challenge in their work. Job specialization was a method devised by managers precisely to help stretch scarce manpower a bit farther by assigning TRs who had completed one job to an essentially similar job, thus requiring less familiarization time and less assistance from managers and other TRs.

Indeed, the job specialization system accomplished what it was intended to accomplish: the TRs were able to handle more work in less time than would otherwise have been possible. But beyond a certain point the system became subtly unproductive and began to create a greater problem than the one it solved. This was because the experience generated by the system was progressively drained of the very elements that had attracted most of the men to this type of work in the first place: the challenge of solving a set of technical riddles and of familiarizing oneself with the link between theory and application in a particular technical setting. Gradually, in other words, the loss of these motivating experiences predisposed the TRs to react one day to a precipitant.

Again it must be stressed that other factors were involved. But in trying to reduce predispositions to unwanted behavior one identifies as many of them as possible and classifies them (roughly, of necessity) according to both potency and accessibility—

how influential are they, and how readily can they be changed? – and then proceeds to attack those whose potency and accessibility are highest. The job specialization system was one of several predisposing factors that met these criteria, and accordingly it was attacked.

It was also defended, and this is a typical problem. The system *was* accomplishing what it was designed to do, and it seemed incredible to those who benefited from it that it was also contributing to a potentially lethal process. The debate within the inner councils of management as to whether to preserve or change the job specialization system was sharp and even acrimonious. When all points had been made and rebutted, the managing director acted boldly. Henceforth, he declared, TRs would be assigned to no more than two essentially similar jobs unless it was with their own consent; and no more than three unless he personally approved.

These and other actions brought the resignation rate back to tolerable levels in a matter of months. It is of course impossible to present an indisputable argument that the actions were responsible for the change. Yet it is certainly unlikely that they made no contribution, and more than likely that their contribution was substantial – and elegant, as well.

THE ANTICIPATION OF POTENTIAL PROBLEMS

Another company which had used attitude surveys to identify the sources of difficulties after they had occurred decided to experiment with an anticipatory survey designed to identify potential trouble before it occurred. They chose a group of clerical and administrative departments in which there were no overt signs of attitude or behavior problems and where management was generally contented with productivity and labor costs. A survey was conducted in a routine way, and it was only when the data were subjected to an intensive statistical analysis that some fascinating patterns began to emerge.

When the data were analyzed according to the sex of the

employees, there was a tendency for the women's attitudes to be somewhat more positive on nearly all questions than the men's. This is a fairly common finding. When the data were analyzed according to length of employment, there was a tendency for attitudes to become progressively more negative as length of employment increased; this too is a fairly common result. But when the data were analyzed simultaneously according to both sex and length of employment, it became clear that the decline of attitudes with length of employment occurred almost entirely among the males. In fact, the decline for males alone was considerably steeper than that for men and women combined.

The differences were not difficult to explain. Ironically, the underlying psychology was the same for both men and women: both were relatively young, moderately educated groups whose interests were largely concerned with the future. For the women, the future looked excellent: marriage within a few years, and in the meantime a pleasant, well-paid interlude. For the men the future looked like an indefinite repetition of the present as promotions from the clerical ranks were rare. Thus work which was tolerable if its end was in sight became much less tolerable if it seemed to lead nowhere. Out of this gradually growing frustration the men acquired a generalized bitterness and antipathy. Those who had been employed for several years were in many cases quite hostile toward the company and felt – vaguely and illogically but still significantly, as far as their behavior was concerned – somehow betrayed.

But the number of such men was small and the overall averages in the attitude data were not bad at all. A superficial analysis would simply have confirmed what was already known: that this was a quiescent, reasonably tranquil group. But in view of the time-lag theory what they *were* was of less significance than what they might become; and accordingly the analysis was pushed farther.

At the time, the ratio of males to females was roughly 3:1, and this seemed likely to increase since the hiring ratio for males was even higher. Further, the ratio of longer-employed to recently-employed males seemed likely to increase, since separations were relatively rare after the first year of employment. Thus it was clear that unless something could be done to relieve the career frustrations of the male clerical workers, the *percentage* of longer-service (therefore, as a rule, disgruntled) workers would also grow.

It does not require a majority to increase labor costs: a substantial minority of negligent, lackadaisical or hostile workers is sufficient for that. And a substantial minority seemed inevitable, since the nature of the work offered relatively few promotional opportunities. Some minor organizational changes were made to increase the number of supervisors, but it was clear that this would not be adequate.

An elegant solution in this case would require that no untoward reactions develop, while at the same time assuring that the work of these departments was done properly. That is, preventive action must be effective without producing unacceptable side-effects. The search for an elegant solution to this latest cost problem led to a re-examination of the premises on which the presumed 'inevitable problem' was based. If the premises were true then the conclusion seemed logical enough. Attitudes would eventually turn sour, no doubt leading to some kind of costly consequence. But were the premises necessarily true? More to the point, what *were* the premises?

One premise that could be challenged, and without which the deduction of 'inevitable problems' was no longer valid, was that the hiring rate had to be higher for males than for females. Upon examination this turned out to be more a matter of custom or preference than necessity. An inventory of all jobs in these departments revealed that while a few had to be done by men (because heavy lifting or night work was involved) and a few had to be done by women (reception work), most jobs could in fact be done by either sex. The higher resignation rate for women (due to marriage, pregnancy or husbands being transferred to another city) had resulted in a tendency for the more complicated jobs to be filled by men because they had more months of experience when openings occurred.

If hiring ratios were changed so that the percentage of women increased, even after the effects of their higher resignation rate, what results could be anticipated? Mathematically, the growth of a 'substantial minority' of career-frustrated males would be delayed if not stopped altogether. The women would continue to leave after a few years, and precisely for that reason would find work that in itself led nowhere tolerable and even enjoyable. The likelihood of deteriorated attitudes and costly behavioral consequences would be greatly diminished. The 'inevitable problem' itself would, in other words, cease to be inevitable.

But what of side-effects? Recruiting and training costs would rise, simply because there would be a more frequent need to replace departed employees. Further, the average experience level would be lower and this would create a need for closer supervision. And some supervisors objected candidly that young women with their sensitivities and emotions were harder to supervise than men. There was, in other words, a cost to the solution, and management was faced with the classical 'trade-off' decision: was the solution worth the cost? Could another solution be found that was acceptably effective and less costly? Did the problem really have to be solved at all? That is, would it be better simply to tolerate it rather than pay the costs of any solution?

In this instance management felt that the costs would, in effect, be an inexpensive form of insurance against an eventuality that was neither improbable nor desirable. Accordingly, hiring ratios were changed and the results were monitored by both productivity measurements and further attitude surveys. Productivity has not suffered and attitudes have actually improved somewhat. In part, the improvement is only a mathematical artifact since more women are included in the survey. Some office wits have suggested that the increased number of charming co-workers has had a beneficial effect on male attitudes. A more serious explanation is that the lower percentage of men reduces the competition for senior clerical assignments (which are still likely, because of length of experience, to go to men), thereby improving their optimism about their careers.

One might argue that the 'inevitable problem' was only a

phantom and would never have occurred anyway. In this case management preferred not to take that risk. It is probably justified in congratulating itself on having achieved the most elegant solution of all: the prevention of a problem that was anticipated in time.

In both of these cases the attitude-survey technique itself was conventional. What was not so conventional was the use to which the data were put, following the time-lag concepts of Likert and the recognition that labor costs are more likely to increase through subtle, unanticipated effects than because of obvious blunders. Thus an old technique, applied in the context of some powerful new concepts derived from the behavioral sciences, has created a much more sophisticated and effective form of labor cost control than was previously possible.

Suggested Reading:

1. LIKERT, R., *The Human Organization: Its Management and Value,* McGraw-Hill, New York, 1967.

CHAPTER 4

The Effects of Work upon Work

FOR many managers the term 'motivation' still connotes traits which are somehow 'built in' to certain individuals, especially desirable traits such as zeal, enthusiasm, determination and an intense commitment to the accomplishment of goals. In other words, either you are 'motivated' or you are not and there is not a great deal that can be done about it, other than sporadically attempting to inspire those who accomplish little to emulate those who accomplish much.

But as more behavioral science research data became available to managers, it became increasingly apparent that the actual behavior of workers could often be best understood as a *reaction* to the situation in which they found themselves, rather than an expression of any inherent traits. In other words, most people are capable of a wide variety of behavior, and their actual conduct in any given situation will depend on the way in which environment draws upon their available 'inventory' of possible responses. Further, the 'environment' had to be understood more broadly: it not only included working conditions, compensation and supervision (the main concerns of the 'benevolent' phase of personnel management), but also the experiences generated by doing the job and the web of communications in which the job was embedded.

Recognizing that behavior is usually a response, rather than an inevitable acting out of some inner drive, managers have become increasingly concerned with the extent to which they can deliberately shape the environment in which the response is made. In other words, they have become more interested in that aspect of motivation which they are in a position to influence (the environment in which workers cope with their assignments) and correspondingly less interested in that aspect over which they can exert relatively little control (the individual's traits and pre-dispositions). Thus, to the behaviorally sophisticated manager, the term 'motivation' is more likely to connote an action or event which produces a change in behavior than a desire by an individual to behave in a particular way.

This is a more pragmatic view of motivation. It is more compatible than the older trait-oriented view with the desire of managers to get down to specifics and cope with tangible problems, and also with the implications of increasingly sophisticated studies in the behavioral sciences. As a result, attention is increasingly focused on the specific *kinds* of on-the-job behavior which can be *influenced by managerial action* and which have a *direct relationship to productivity*.

It has been recognized that some forms of on-the-job behavior can be influenced by managerial action in more or less direct, readily understood ways; while others can be influenced only subtly and indirectly. It is also clear that both desirable and undesirable forms of behavior can be motivated by managerial actions, and that in this sense motivation is neither positive nor negative, but simply refers to actions which cause behavior to change.

'BAD' BEHAVIOR – A REACTION TO DULL WORK

Among the actions which appear to be susceptible to managerial influence and which bear a fairly direct, common-sense relationship to labor costs are absenteeism, resignations and the frequency of errors. Studies of absenteeism and resignation suggest that they are often simply different ways to cope with essentially the same problem, which is unattractive work. The more mobile or 'marketable' individual will leave such work altogether in hopes of greater stimulation or at least variety elsewhere, while his less bold or less sought-after counterpart must satisfy himself with periodic self-decreed 'vacations' in the form of absenteeism. The underlying need in both cases is for escape.

It is not stretching a point too far to suggest that the same basic need is at the root of many errors, since these are usually due to attention lapses rather than to inability. Attention to work which is neither enjoyable nor unpredictable is extraordinarily difficult for most people to maintain. Thus availability for work and attention to work, both of which figure heavily in labor costs, are both influenced to a significant degree by the reaction of the worker to the work itself.

SOCIAL ORIGINS OF THE CHANGE IN ATTITUDES TO WORK

Many managers find this difficult to comprehend, yet if they are ever to get their labor costs under effective control it is essential that they do so. They may object that the men are fairly paid and decently treated and that while the work may not be diverting it is necessary and deserving of proper effort; all of which may be true but also, alas, irrelevant. The problem, which will almost inevitably become substantially more severe in the coming decade, is once again an unanticipated side-effect; this time of the enormous success which the present generation of senior managers have made of their enterprises and therefore of the economy. Unemployment on the scale that makes men enduringly appreciative of any job at all has not been seen since the onset of the Second World War, and purchasing power has risen to such levels that the better part of the population is really more concerned with indulgences than with necessities.

Dramatic evidence that the specter of unemployment no longer had its former disciplinary power over workers was obtained by American automobile manufacturers during the economic recession of 1970–71 when, despite national unemployment levels that sometimes exceeded 6 per cent, absenteeism from assembly line jobs also set records, sometimes exceeding 13 per cent.

More importantly, educational levels (paid for chiefly by taxes and therefore based ultimately upon the condition of the economy) have risen dramatically. At the time of writing, the *median* educational level of the employed US labor force is twelve years: that is, *one out of two American workers has completed* more *than twelve years of formal schooling.* This figure will inevitably rise since the workers leaving the labor force through retirement or death have a much lower average educational level than the younger workers who enter the labor force to replace them. Similar trends are at work in most European countries as a result of educational reforms introduced in the post-war era. The results are now beginning to be felt by industry in the form of sharp differences in the capabilities, and more importantly in the attitudes toward work, between older workers who are the products of a pre-war educational system and younger workers whose talents have, on average, benefited from much fuller development. In general the younger worker is less docile, less appreciative of steady employment and social benefits, and more prone to absenteeism, turnover and strikes than his older counterpart is or was at the same age. This trend is likely to continue simply because the educational reforms cannot be abandoned. Inevitably, during the decade of the 1970s industry must begin massive adjustments to a wholly new type of labor force.

In sum, during the working lifetime of most senior managers a virtual revolution has taken place among the forces that largely shape attitudes toward work, and the principal if unintended revolutionists have been the senior managers themselves since they have created the prosperity and supported the educational reforms. (As an aside I might comment that to enjoy to the utmost the times we live in one must really cultivate a taste for irony.)

HERZBERG AND THE EFFECT OF WORK ON MOTIVATION

Frederick Herzberg, who is Professor of Industrial Psychology at the University of Utah, has made the most substantial contribution to the analysis of the motivational effect of work. In a well-known series of experiments beginning in the late 1950s, Herzberg and his associates drew a distinction between two kinds of motivational influences which seemed to have markedly different effects on behavior and performance. The first they called *hygiene factors*, since they were essentially aspects of the working environment which, when ineffectively administered, resulted in resentful attitudes and diminished effort or even hostile acts against the organization; but which when effectively administered resulted in a more or less neutral reaction, without any marked or lasting enthusiasm for the work or increase in productivity. The term 'hygiene' was used because the effect is essentially the same as that achieved by public health measures such as water purification, which in itself does not make people healthier, but failure to give proper attention to it could endanger the health of many. Herzberg included among hygiene factors most of the elements traditionally emphasized by personnel departments: pay, social benefits, supervisory styles and policies, and physical working conditions.

The other set of influences were called *motivators*, since they seemed to produce lasting satisfaction and commitment of the individual's energies to the job. These were experiences generated by work which were sufficiently challenging to engage the bulk of the individual's abilities and included a sense of accomplishment, a sense of increasing mastery of competence, of recognition through increased responsibility.

In one sense, the term 'motivators' is a bit unfortunate since Herzberg uses it in a more restricted sense than do most behavioral scientists. This has led to some avoidable but vigorous controversies, such as the question 'Is money a motivator?' If we accept Herzberg's definition, money is usually a hygiene factor and not a motivator; but if by 'motivator' we mean something that influences behavior, then money clearly is a motivator, especially of membership, that is, willingness to be hired and to remain in the employ of a given organization. Its influence on productivity is not marked except as a negative influence in the case of inequitable payment. However, more than semantics is involved in the controversy over Herzberg's work.

There are two basic reasons why Herzberg's work has attracted so much attention. First, it calls into question the efficacy of most of the traditional practises of personnel departments with respect to motivation; and second, Herzberg concludes that satisfaction and dissatisfaction are not opposites but entirely distinct and independent feelings. With regard to the former, Herzberg holds that hygiene factors cannot be dispensed with, and indeed require constant skilled administrative attention; but that it would be unrealistic to expect them to generate commitment or enthusiasm. The best that can be expected is a lack of negative attitudes. Positive attitudes toward work, if they are to occur at all, are more likely to be the result of building 'motivators' (in Herzberg's sense) into the job. With regard to the relationship of satisfaction and dissatisfaction, this is a theoretical point of greater interest to academicians than to practitioners or managers. The methods by which Herzberg's experiments were designed and by which the statistical results were interpreted have been questioned by some academicians, resulting in a lengthy series of articles in professional journals that have little or no relevance to management problems but have generated considerable heat, some of which has come to the attention of managers.

JOB ENRICHMENT

The best-known application of Herzberg's work has been the 'job enrichment' experiments carried out in certain units of the American Telephone and Telegraph Company and of Imperial Chemical Industries in the United Kingdom. These involved re-designing jobs in such a way as to eliminate or at least reduce the amount of time spent in essentially dull, unstimulating tasks; by incorporating into a single job related tasks previously separated into several jobs, so as to provide clear responsibility on the part of each individual for a definable unit or sub-unit of work; and the addition of more challenging responsibilities related to the work, such as scheduling, setting priorities and on-the-spot decisions related to the product or process with which the work was involved. These experiments indicate a promising opportunity for applying the job enrichment technique to the reduction of labor turnover and absenteeism and to the improvement of quality and efficiency.

The severity of these problems, especially absenteeism, has recently reached unprecedented levels in American industry and especially that sector of industry where reliance on assembly line procedures has denuded most jobs of opportunities for achievement, responsibility or growth. James Roche, former chief executive officer of the largest manufacturing company in the United States (General Motors), recently commented:

We've got absenteeism in our plants, which is common throughout the industry, running twice as high as it did a few years ago . . . You can't run a business on this basis, effectively or efficiently, because the two highest days in the week for absenteeism are Fridays and Mondays. So, absenteeism of 13 per cent to 15 per cent is fairly common. Well, when you get ready to start an assembly line at eight o'clock in the morning and you find out that you have 13 per cent of the people gone, you have to do a lot of scrounging. You have to bring people over to try to man the stations who are not proficient or who have not had the experience. You've got to double your supervision, you've got to double your inspection, and this creates an insurmountable burden.

(*Business Week*, 11 July 1970)

To some American behavioral scientists, the failure of many managements to anticipate or cope successfully with increasing problems of worker non-availability was in part due to a failure of behavioral science itself; or rather the result of an excessive preoccupation with management technology to the comparative neglect of the experience of actual work. Professor Marvin Dunnette of the University of Minnesota has observed that

the first widely publicized inkling that men and women work for more than money was, of course, based on findings from the famous Western Electric Hawthorne experiments. Nearly every study, review, or new theory of work motivation since then has emphasized that people value certain job dimensions such as achievements (accomplishment), responsibility, recognition, and liking the work (work itself) more than certain other job dimensions such as raw money (money itself), favorable physical conditions in the work place, nice company policies and practices, and good supervision.

Startlingly, in spite of all this emphasis over these many decades on the motivational importance of liking one's job and sensing fulfillment from it, companies have allowed a large majority of jobs, particularly those capable of being rationalized and routinized, to be virtually denuded of diversity and of the critically important elements of job interest, responsibility, feedback, and recognition. It is to the discredit of many, if not most, industrial psychologists practicing during the 1940s and 1950s that they placed so much emphasis on improving personnel selection to the near exclusion of improving individual opportunities for making wise job decisions or of changing jobs to fit individuals better. The 1940s and 1950s were an era devoted almost solely to measuring the shapes of people (pegs) for the purpose of estimating how well they might fit the shapes of jobs (holes) available in industry . . .

Psychologists emphasizing individualized career guidance or job counseling were strangely absent from industrial settings during those years. Even more serious, nearly all vocational guidance in high schools and colleges was directed toward that small minority of college-bound students possessing measured aptitudes suggesting they could enter white collar and professional occupations . . .

So the 'establishment' of industrial psychology did nearly nothing during those years of the 1940s and 1950s to promote approaches that might help persons in the so-called lower level jobs get more from their jobs. This practice gained further academic and industrial support, apparently, from the large number of rather poorly conceptualized field research studies showing very little relationship between job satisfaction and job productivity.

(From a review by M. D. Dunnette of
'Motivation Through the Work Itself',
Journal of Professional Psychology, 1970.)

Professor Dunnette's observations with regard to job enrichment serve to stress an extremely important point which all managers interested in practical applications of scientific findings would do well to remember: all scientists (including the behavioral variety) are human and therefore their work is subject to the same variations that affect other human activities such as fashions, periods of underemphasis and overemphasis, and disagreements that generate more heat than light. Therefore it is necessary for managers to follow the scientific literature or at least delve into it from time to time. The manager who finds this discipline too taxing should perhaps avoid the behavioral sciences altogether since he has no effective protection against being swayed by momentary fads or one-sided views of complicated problems. Behavioral science is evolving, not static; and given the complexity of its subject it is unlikely to reach a static condition during the lifetime of any manager reading these lines. I might add that the manager who lacks the time or inclination to follow behavioral science developments is, no doubt inadvertently, guaranteeing his own eventual obsolescence.

Another poorly conceptualized objection, in my opinion, is the view that to apply the job enrichment principle broadly would quickly cause more trouble than its gains would be worth since most people would soon find themselves well beyond their 'levels of incompetence' and therefore subject to errors and gross mishandling of their responsibilities. Upon examination this does not turn out to be a serious problem. Most errors are due to inattention rather than to incompetence, and inattention is more likely to be due to boredom or disinterest than to being overwhelmed by excessive responsibility. In a word, overcompetence is already the source of far more errors than incompetence is ever likely to cause.

The best defense against pushing people beyond their depth is to temper one's enthusiasm for the job enrichment method by introducing it gradually to each individual, and to regard anyone's 'level of incompetence' (should job enrichment carry him beyond his abilities) as a temporary barrier rather than a permanent limit. The temporary nature of most incompetencies is perhaps most easily demonstrated by the fact that you were once incompetent to read this book, just as I was once incompetent to write it. The gradual growth of competence, *given the opportunity to grow*, is far more characteristic of most human natures than any unbreachable limits.

SUCCESSES OF JOB ENRICHMENT

In one large American aerospace company, this growth of competence was dramatically illustrated by an experiment in which a group of machinists were given virtually full control over their own scheduling, production methods and inspection procedures. In effect they became their own supervisors and technical advisers, which was all the more remarkable since prior to the experiment the group had an unfortunate record of slow-downs, grievances and equipment failures. Production initially fell, which is normal with any change, and then rose to much higher levels than had previously been thought possible. But it is in qualitative rather than quantitative changes that the full dimensions of growth became apparent.

For example, these men have been known to form 'delegations' and to call on the supervisors of departments that supply them with raw materials, in order to complain (sometimes vociferously) about late delivery and poor quality. Or they have been seen coming to work one shift early for the purpose of exchanging information with the men who operate their equipment on the previous shift. In a word, they are acting like managers and showing all the signs of entrepreneurial pride, which no doubt has a great deal to do with the increased production rate. Apparently job enrichment taps a strong motivational source in many people, which is their desire to be as much as possible the masters of what they are doing.

THE RESISTANCE OF MANAGERS THEMSELVES

However, job enrichment does raise some problems. These will be reviewed more extensively in the final chapter, which is devoted to attempting to anticipate the future. For the moment we might note that if the fullest release of talent for productive purposes is obtainable through making the job more challenging and turning the worker, in effect, into as much of a 'self-manager' as we can make of him, then the principal limitation upon our ability to accomplish such a change is the motivation of managers. Paradoxically, it is less comfortable and perhaps even less enjoyable to manage an organization whose employees are fully motivated than one in which they are disinterested and apathetic.

Thus the real test to which job enrichment has yet to be put is the one which management itself has not yet faced: the compatibility of managerial comfort in its power prerogatives with the highest productivity and creativity of which men in general appear to be capable.

Suggested Reading:

1. FORD, R. N., *Motivation through the Work Itself*, American Management Association, New York, 1969.
2. PAUL, W. J., JR, ROBERTSON, K., and HERZBERG, F., 'Job Enrichment Pays Off', *Harvard Business Review*, vol. 47, no. 2, March–April 1969.

CHAPTER 5

The Effects of Behavior upon Behavior

In seeking to influence human behavior the realist will be most interested in measures over which he can exert some degree of control and whose effects are substantial. Both effect *and* control must be considered. Some of our more lingering myths about measures of influence are based on excessive fascination with effects to the neglect of such practical considerations as control.

Consider, for example, money: when provided in sufficiently lavish sums it can produce some remarkable, if temporary, changes in behavior; and for this reason some managers plead with their financial controllers for greater liberality in wage budgets as if that would somehow 'motivate' their subordinates to heroic levels of proficiency. Unfortunately, money (that is, increases in current income) has some of the characteristics of a woman who is beautiful but dull: the prospect is tantalizing but one tires quickly of the reality and begins to seek new diversions.

LIMITATIONS OF MONEY AS A MOTIVATOR

The short-lived nature of most monetary satisfactions is the basis of another of those delicious ironies with which behavioral research seems to abound: the principal constraint on our ability to motivate with money is not psychological but financial. Pay increases on the scale and with the frequency necessary to maintain a state of monetary bliss would quickly bankrupt most corporate treasuries, and it is questionable whether blissful workers would be significantly more productive than those who were simply resigned to economic realities. The irony is that money is the most expensive motivator and this rather than indifference to money is the main reason why it has limited effectiveness.

Management simply cannot control enough money to use it other than as a price for labor (although it should be noted in passing that failure to pay an equitable price brings severe and richly deserved penalties).

BEHAVIOR AS A REACTION TO OTHER BEHAVIOR

Turning from influential measures we cannot adequately control, to those we can at least hope to control, behavioral scientists have become increasingly fascinated with the effect of behavior itself upon behavior; that is, with the extent to which actions are largely explicable as *re*actions to what other people do. Most of us are highly sensitive to each other, in terms of our overt behavior if not our discernment. To cite a trivial but common example, if someone speaks to you and looks directly into your eyes, it would usually be difficult to avoid his gaze if only because it would be such an obvious attempt to break contact. You may not want to give him as much attention as he demands, but to withdraw it would seem discourteous or even cowardly, and for the sake of avoiding either implication you may prefer to endure him until he blinks, or some small noise provides an excuse for you to look away. During those few seconds he will have managed, perhaps inadvertently, to control at least that part of your behavior that involved your eyes.

More substantially, behavioral scientists have become concerned with what they call *assumptions* and *self-fulfilling prophecies*, both concepts deriving from the work of the late Douglas McGregor (who until his death in 1964 was Professor of Industrial Administration at the Massachusetts Institute of Technology). By 'assumptions' is meant the premises or beliefs on which behavior is based. Usually these are unexamined and for that matter unconscious, not in the Freudian sense of being inaccessible, but simply outside awareness because there is so little reason for directing attention to them. When you take your meal at a restaurant it is presumably in the belief that the food was prepared under sanitary conditions, but since you are unlikely to

53

inspect the kitchen the only indication you might have that your assumption was incorrect would be a pain in the stomach afterwards. Obviously assumptions of this kind are necessary if one is to get on with the everyday business of life. We learn from experience that assumptions are occasionally wrong and we simply put up with that because it would be paralytically costly to check all of them.

But some assumptions are very much worth the trouble of checking, especially if you are a manager and therefore charged with accomplishing your work through other people's efforts. These concern your expectations of the people with whom you work, and more specifically your beliefs about their ability, responsibility and trustworthiness. This is one of the many points at which the behavioral sciences clash with entrenched managerial dogma, in this case with the notion that an experienced manager 'knows his men' and therefore can elicit the best behavior that is in them. Probably no one knows anyone else encyclopedically; most of us have broader repertoires than we employ in any one relationship, and in any one relationship we employ that part of our repertoire which seems most appropriate to us. Therefore the behavior that I encounter in you is that part of your repertoire which I (or the situation of which I am a part) elicit from you. In effect I am blinded by my own effect upon you to your potentialities for behaving in other than the ways I see. There is nothing the least bit abnormal about this; on the contrary it is a natural, but not inevitable, result of the way we experience each other and in a statistical sense it is very 'normal' indeed. But it is also a great handicap for a manager (and no doubt other people too, but it is managers with whom we are most concerned here). The worst difficulty is in the effect known as the 'self-fulfilling prophecy', in which experience 'confirms' one's preconceptions because we actually tend to inhibit, or at least not to be impressed by, the actions of others that are inconsistent with our own beliefs about them. In this way we tend willy-nilly to become parts of a pre-programmed charade, and experience fails to teach us anything because we, through our own consistency, standardize it, and ignore or dismiss deviations from the standard (someone else's attempt to introduce an 'inconsistent' part of his own repertoire into his relationship with us). The villain in all this is that same economizing of time which disinclines us to examine our assumptions, and perhaps also a certain unbecoming, but common, self-righteousness which makes us seek elsewhere than in ourselves the cause of such difficulties as we may encounter.

HOW ASSUMPTIONS IMPAIR EFFECTIVE MANAGEMENT

If assumptions and self-fulfilling prophecies only blinded men to each other's potentialities, we might lament that briefly and then get on with more practical things. But their effects are more than abstract, and such 'practical things' as profit-and-loss statements may easily be involved. It is precisely our tendency to inhibit each other and to limit each other to fractions of our behavioral repertoires that locks us into ultimately unprofitable managerial practices (such as the use of fear and coercion), because our truncated and filtered 'experience' suggests that they are the best ways, or indeed the only ways, to get people to work. And it is precisely our inability, or rather our disinclination, to step outside ourselves long enough to examine the adequacy of our assumptions, and the effects that our own assumption-shaped behavior has upon other people's behavior, which insulates us against the potential lessons which our own experiences could teach us. Assumptions make us prematurely old in the sense of using what we already know or think we know as a barrier to further knowledge. In a manager, this common tendency to overvalue one's impressions of others creates resistance to (or worse still, ignorance of) new and possibly useful approaches to his job. In brief, the natural tendency to form and cling to assumptions about other people is, in an age of rapid and even escalating changes of all kinds, an almost certain prescription for managerial obsolescence.

Thus behavioral scientists and managers concerned with finding practical ways to make changes happen have increasingly been drawn together. Their concern is with the viability of the organization itself, which demands not only adaptability from ordinary people (whose path of least resistance lies in being static), but also a flowering of whatever latent talent any of them may possess. This attempt to make organizations facilitors rather than inhibitors of accomplishment is known as organization development. At the time of writing this it is more of a program than a coherent group of tested techniques; one might almost say it is a diagnosis in search of a prescription.

ORGANIZATION DEVELOPMENT

Unlike personnel selection and attitude surveys which have established technologies, organization development is currently one of the frontier areas of behavioral science. It is at the stage where critics need little talent to carp with its results. Perhaps it is fair to say at present that organization development is more important for what it is attempting than for what it has done. In the balance of this chapter we will be concerned with some examples of how the attempt is being made.

SENSITIVITY TRAINING AND ITS LIMITATIONS

Historically, organization development was an outgrowth of earlier work on individual development; but more specifically of methods designed to increase one's awareness of the effects of his behavior on other people and of the significance of their behavior toward him. Known generically as sensitivity training, these methods enjoyed a flowering of popularity in the late 1960s and continue to be very much in vogue. However it was a recognition of some of their limitations that led to the attempt to grapple with organizational (as distinguished from individual) effectiveness. Among these were the rapid fading of whatever obvious effects sensitivity training had upon individual behavior, and the difficulty in demonstrating any lasting or significant influence of sensitivity training on the effectiveness of the organization as a whole.

MASS SENSITIVITY TRAINING

The conclusion was drawn that sensitivity training was in some respects an initiation into an unfamiliar culture; one in which candor, openness and mutual helpfulness were the predominant values; and that to return to one's 'native' culture (i.e. the organization) after a brief sojourn in sensitivity would inevitably lead to a re-adoption of safe and familiar ways. That is, the transplanted behavior would not survive for long in an unprepared and therefore unreceptive environment. Thus the earliest attempts at organization development were essentially attempts to use sensitivity training within a given organization on a larger scale than before. In some respects this was not unlike trying to make the disease respond to the available medicine. Not surprisingly, when 'organization development' is in fact a euphemism for mass sensitivity training the results are not unlike those of mass baptism: there are some zealous converts, some people who have learned a new vocabulary and little else, and quite a few people who are not entirely sure what the ritual was all about except that they enjoyed it.

The more sophisticated approaches to organization development stress diagnosis as a prerequisite to treatment and a deliberate attempt to change the 'culture' of an organization sufficiently to make the transplanted, newly learned skills of candor, etc., self-reinforcing and therefore more likely to become permanent.

THE DIAGNOSTIC APPROACH

The basic premises of the diagnostic approach to organization development are that organizations differ sufficiently to require a tailored approach with specific improvement objectives (as distinguished from putting everyone through the same standard exercises); and that people are more likely to collaborate with an improvement program they have in effect helped to design than with one which has been created for them. The 'medicine' that is eventually prescribed may or may not include some variant of sensitivity training. In fact it usually does, but this is not inevitable, and what is more important is that the training efforts are not diffuse but are targetted to producing specific changes in specific relationships.

Four main diagnostic approaches are in use in the United States today. One is the 'Profile of Organization Characteristics' developed by Rensis Likert and his associates at the University of Michigan. Essentially a research instrument, this is a fifty-item questionnaire in which managers record their impressions of the management systems actually in use in their companies. Analysis of the consensus of replies can help to indicate in what ways the organization enhances, and in what ways it inhibits, the accomplishments of its members. Another diagnostic method is incorporated in the 'managerial grid' exercises developed by Robert Blake and Jane Mouton of Scientific Methods, Inc. This is an integrated series of questionnaires and demonstrations designed to reveal the relative degree of emphasis given by managements to human and economic considerations. A third approach was developed by Gordon L. Lippitt and Warren H. Schmidt; it is a series of questionnaires linked to their theory of the stages of organizational growth. Lippitt and Schmidt attempt to enable managers to discern the degree of maturity their *organization* (not the managers themselves) has reached and the specific problems that stand in the way of further development.

SELF-DIAGNOSIS

A fourth approach is essentially a self-diagnosing matrix; it is a strategy for gathering and analyzing relevant data rather than a questionnaire approach. As used by the author and others, it consists of a series of confidential interviews with a group of managers whose jobs require them to interact; for reasons which will be apparent in a moment it is not feasible to include more than a dozen or so managers in any given matrix. The subject of each of these interviews is the manager's candid perceptions of each of the other managers in the group; more specifically of what he feels they *do* that enhances or limits his effectiveness, or what they do not do which might help to make him more effective. The interviewer maintains the focus upon behavior rather than on general impressions, and on job-relevant behavior rather than on more diffuse likes or dislikes. (The latter are excluded because they are usually difficult or even impossible to do very much about.) The number of perceptions to be analyzed is equal to the number of managers in the group squared, minus the number in the group, which is why analytical difficulties increase geometrically with the addition of more managers to any given matrix.

The matrix itself is analyzed in several ways. Reading all perceptions of any given individual reveals the consensus impression(s) – sometimes there are more than one – of him; in effect we can look at him through the collective eyes of his peers and study the impact his behavior has upon them. Using their observations (rather than the interviewer's) as the criterion, we can explore their implications for questions that are directly relevant to the prescriptive stage of organizational development, such as:

Is his contribution to the effectiveness of the others in the group seen, on the whole, as positive, negative or simply lacking?

Does it appear that he is open enough to consider some possibly unflattering observations about himself constructively, without becoming defensive?

Does he seem adaptable enough to undertake, and persist in, a conscious attempt to alter certain habit patterns?

Is he evidently integrated enough to withstand a certain amount of candid criticism without being panicked or feeling forever wounded?

What would be realistic, attainable targets (in terms of deliberate self-modification of overt behavior patterns) for him that

would, if attained, increase his contribution to the others sufficiently to be worth the costs of time, money and personal strain
that might be involved?

Note that the prescriptive phase is intended to modify what
people do, not what they think; ideas are altered (if at all) by
experience and not by 'brainwashing' or other arcane techniques.

PRESCRIBING TREATMENT – 'TEAM BUILDING'

Considering all these inferred diagnoses together, an estimate can
be made of whether any kind of 'treatment' is desirable, or
feasible, at all; and if so what methods would be best suited to the
needs and limitations of the group. Sometimes what is required is
not training, but an organization change; sometimes training will
be designed for some people but not for others in order to protect
them from more stress than they could handle or simply to avoid
a high probability of futility. Sometimes the existing relationships
will be as close to optimum already as one could reasonably wish,
so that intervention would be pointless.

But most of the time, when some attainable and potentially
worthwhile gains appear to be in prospect, a series of 'team
building' sessions will be designed to help the group achieve
them. These may involve individual counselling or group inter-
changes or both. The methods used are less important than their
insistent focus upon current and recent overt behavior as the sole
topics for discussion, and upon helpfulness rather than recrimina-
tion as the sole legitimate motive for speaking. By comparison
with the completely unstructured approach of sensitivity training,
this method requires the individual to involve considerably less
than his full unfettered self; it is less revealing and therefore more
like the ordinary social reality to which we are all accustomed. It
attempts less than sensitivity training and for that reason, perhaps
paradoxically, it is likely to accomplish more of what it sets out to
accomplish. This more structured and limited approach to
behavior modification is sometimes known as team building.

Perhaps the most important characteristic of any attempt at behavior modification is that it must be repetitive. The effects of *any* effort to change adult behavior patterns are unlikely to persist if only one dose (or a few widely separated doses) are provided; even with good training and the best of intentions, the effects of a few weeks are no match for the sheer inertia of decades of learning to be what the person already is. Consequently team building has its best chance of success when provided in brief but relatively frequent doses. As an aside, it might be noted that one of the major handicaps of sensitivity training as it is ordinarily practised is that it takes so long to produce its effects (two weeks is usually considered an appropriate dosage), that it is uneconomical to repeat very often or even at all. Thus sensitivity training has so to speak, numerous graduates but relatively few 'post-graduates'. However, even the less stringent economics of team building can become prohibitive in time. Thus if the effort is to yield more than temporary benefits it is essential that a means be found to make its effects self-perpetuating. The interventions must eventually cease and if only for this reason the individuals involved must not become dependent upon a particular technique in order to enhance each other's effectiveness.

MAKING 'GOOD' BEHAVIOR HABITUAL

Perhaps the most practical solution to this difficult problem is to achieve what might be called a 'critical mass'; that is, to have enough interventions occur frequently enough with a large enough participation of the organization's management that the behavior encountered in the training sessions (candor, helpfulness, etc.) becomes, in effect, a part of the organization's on-going culture. The members of the organization become dedicated to making each other more effective, not because they take vows to do so but because it becomes a habit and also because it is expected of them. Something like this happy state of affairs actually seems to have developed in a number of American firms which have made sufficiently massive, persistent and skilled efforts at organization development. (An example is TRW Systems, a large aerospace company in California.) However, these companies are exceptions rather than the norm and even within them one finds pockets, as it were, of mutual inhibition; but on the whole they stand as encouraging demonstrations that most men are at their best when trying to bring out the best in each other.

Thus it appears to be possible to do something that is significant and useful about the effects of behavior on behavior. But the record is not yet long enough or clear enough to warrant hopes for dramatic breakthroughs. In its present condition, the importance of organization development lies more in its recognition of a need and its experimental approach to behavior modification than in its concrete achievements.

Suggested Reading:

1. MCGREGOR, D., *The Professional Manager* (eds. Warren G. Bennis and Caroline McGregor), McGraw-Hill, New York, 1967.
2. LIKERT, R., *The Human Organization: Its Management and Value*, McGraw-Hill, New York, 1967.
3. BLAKE, R. R., and MOUTON, J. S., *The Managerial Grid*, Gulf Publishing, Houston, Texas, 1964.
4. LIPPITT, G. L., and SCHMIDT, W. H., 'Crises in a Developing Organization', *Harvard Business Review*, vol. 45, no. 6, November–December 1967.
5. BECKHARD, R., *Organization Development*, Addison-Wesley, 1969.
6. BENNIS, W. G., *Organization Development: Its Nature, Origins and Prospects*, Addison-Wesley, 1969.
7. BRADFORD, GIBB and BENNE, *T-group Theory and Laboratory Method: Innovation in Re-Education*, Wiley, 1964.
8. SMITH, P. B., *Improving Skills in Working with People: The T-group*, HMSO, 1969.

CHAPTER 6

Some Crystal-Ball Gazing

WE are usually too preoccupied with the present, or worse still
with a nostalgic misinterpretation of the present, to anticipate the
future and prepare for it. The dilemma is as old as mankind, and
it would hardly be surprising if it lasts as long as mankind. But if
that part of mankind which is charged with deciding how resources and effort will be expended (namely, management) were
to become a bit more expert in coping with the future, mankind
might last a little longer and man's institutions might serve him a
little better. If this can be done at all, it would require that we
identify those events which have already taken place which are
also perhaps more likely than the other events of our times to
exert a shaping influence on the future.

In other words, you select premises and proceed to draw
deductions from them. Whether your selection is accurate or not
time alone will tell; but if both your selection and your logic are
reasonably astute, the deductions need not be too wide of the
ultimate mark. In applying this method to trying to forecast the
managerial environment of, say, the next eight to ten years
(which is about as far ahead as I think this method can be sensibly
applied), we are doing nothing more than projecting the process
of historical analysis forward. In other words, instead of trying
to identify events in the remote past which had a shaping influence on the more recent past, we look for potentially porten-
tous recent events and project their probable consequences.

I have tried to do this only in the context of those problems
that I have studied intensively enough to feel some competence
with, namely the utilization of human talent and the administration of large industrial organizations, both in North America and
Western Europe. My guess is that two sets of events are going to
exert a shaping influence on the managerial climate of these

regions in the near future. These are the continuing social and economic changes which alter the values of the younger part of the labor force, and the growing impact of the behavioral sciences on managerial practices.

THE CHANGING VALUES OF EMPLOYEES

The character of the labor force has always changed from year to year as young people enter it and older people leave it. However, during the last decade, the rate of change has accelerated due to pronounced differences between the entrants and the leavers. While in any one year the change may not be sufficient to notice, over a period of, say, five years the changes can be quite marked.

Thus in companies which have been expanding rapidly and therefore have a relatively high proportion of younger employees, it would not be uncommon at all to find that a majority of them are not particularly impressed by employment security, steady incomes, or even so called 'merit' systems of wage or salary progression. Some of the more idealistic ones are increasingly concerned about what effect their jobs have upon society or the environment. Most of them, idealistic or not, are increasingly concerned about what the job does for *them* in terms of developing their talents and providing them with opportunities to take charge of their own careers.

In other words, our industrial organizations are being increasingly populated by careerists, especially in that part of the organization on whom its fortunes will increasingly depend: the professional and managerial groups. However, even at 'blue collar' levels, the difference between generations is noticeable. The younger worker is less patient, less willing to trade immediate financial gain for security, and in fact is increasingly restive with the seniority system itself.

The forces which have produced these changes are still with us and show no signs of declining permanently. These are the continued growth of the economy and above all the constantly increasing educational level. Therefore there is every reason to believe that these trends will continue into the foreseeable future. An economic 'recession', at least of the sort we have seen since the Second World War, is not sufficient to arrest this process; although a full-scale 'depression' of the order of 1934 might do so.

Management is becoming increasingly 'behavioral science minded' for two reasons. The first is that the behavioral sciences themselves have begun to do relevant work on practical managerial problems and to translate the implications of this research into languages that managers can grasp readily. But perhaps a more important reason is that the upper echelons of management are being increasingly penetrated by the generation of managers which got its university training after the Second World War and is much more receptive than previous generations of managers to ideas that have academic or scientific origins. Their interest in applying what essentially is a systems approach to the human problems of management will undoubtedly continue.

Assuming that these events (which are already history rather than prophecy) will actually have a shaping influence on the future, what are the consequences we can expect?

TOMORROW'S PROBLEMS

One is that sooner or later, some company somewhere is going to succeed in getting most of its employees highly motivated. While their productivity, and especially their creativity, is likely to be extraordinary, so are the managerial problems they will cause. In fact one could argue that it is a great deal easier to manage an essentially unmotivated organization than one whose members are all highly motivated, if only because we have had more practise at the former than the latter.

If the behavioral scientists are right about what unlocks human talent and energy, then many of these highly motivated people are going to be participating actively in the management of their own work, and some could only be described as 'self managers'. This will require quite an adjustment for many of them, but not

65

nearly as severe as that which will be demanded of their superiors. They will then have to cope with the intriguing question: what does a manager do when he no longer has to do his subordinates' thinking for them? Some managers will no doubt welcome the relief from routine scheduling and approvals and will be able to concentrate wholly on planning, coordination, and above all on teaching (which looms as the critical new requirement for effective management in the years ahead). However, others will not be so lucky, and in fact some sizeable shakeouts in management are likely, precisely because effectively motivated employees will reveal all too starkly what kind of people have been promoted into management in the past.

Far too many got into managerial positions for reasons which, if they ever had any relevance, are certainly irrelevant now. Many were promoted on the basis of what was essentially product knowledge to do a quality-control job. Many were promoted on the basis of 'leadership qualities' to do what was essentially a behavior-control job, that is, keeping subordinates in line. Many were promoted simply because they were the 'next in line' themselves. Those managers with nothing more to offer to management than this will find that the rules of the game have been changed on them, and that they have in fact become redundant.

Thus the essential obsolescence of many managerial practises (and unfortunately of many managers as well) may become all too clear in the years ahead. But other problems could be even more severe. Absenteeism from mass production industries is likely to increase. (As previously noted, during the US recession of 1970–71, absenteeism in automobile plants actually rose despite comparatively high unemployment rates and a well-published 'softness' in the economy as a whole.) Voluntary turnover (resignations), while more likely to be dampened when hiring is retarded, is probably heading for higher levels than ever in the longer term. One might almost say that a prolonged period of vocational nomadism among the young (and even the not-so-young) is likely to become the norm.

... AND THEIR SOLUTION

But the vision of the future provided by the present is not entirely apocalyptic. If management will be beset with unprecedented problems, it will also be better equipped for coping with the problems of its day than any previous generation of managers. The university business schools are producing a growing number of professionally trained younger managers. Perhaps even more important is the proliferation of management development programs within companies. While some of these have been criticized (too often justly) for following fads and putting people through available courses rather than determining their training *needs*, by and large management development represents a realistic commitment to a perpetual educational process. In today's world, education ends when life ends, and vice versa.

CASE STUDIES

The papers included here refer specifically to previous chapters:

1. Application of the Personnel Development Series in Europe – Chapter 2

2. Why Managers Don't Use Attitude Survey Results – Chapter 3

3. A Participative Approach to Management *and*

4. Job Enrichment: What Are the Obstacles? – Chapter 4

5. Building More Effective Teams – Chapter 5

CASE STUDY 1

The author of the following article is Dr Harry Laurent, an American psychologist who has spent the bulk of his career as an internal consultant to various affiliates of Standard Oil Company (New Jersey). He was a key member of the team that developed the PDS in the United States, and for the last few years has been located in London where his responsibilities include advising the company's European affiliates on the use of this system. This paper was originally written for internal use within the company and has been edited and reproduced with the permission of Dr Laurent and Esso Europe, Inc.

Application of the
Personnel Development Series in Europe

by Harry Laurent, Esso Europe Inc.

MOST companies rely primarily on sources outside the individual for information about employees' potential for managerial positions. This method has not been completely unsuccessful. Capable people do emerge from the group, and we have been able to fill our managerial positions. However, there are some who argue that the job of a manager is becoming so complex and the need for managers is so urgent that we must start making available to promising employees as soon as possible the opportunity to obtain the training and experience they will need to qualify for management positions and that, therefore, we cannot sit back and wait for the emergence process to operate. We must actively seek out high-level talent and put it to work.

There is some evidence which indicates that the outside source of information is not completely adequate to do the job of identifying management potential during the early years of a man's employment:

Evaluations of management potential are dependent upon individual and local standards. Managers in some locations tend to rate high, others to rate low, and still others tend to give average ratings to most of their people. It is extremely difficult to establish company-wide standards.

For short-service employees the ratings of potential made in one year do not agree very well with ratings made the previous year. In some organizations in which this problem has been investigated the findings indicate that until the men have been observed for six or seven years the ratings are not very stable.

The potential for advancement of young employees tends to be underevaluated or evaluated as average. There is an understandable tendency for a manager to avoid going out on a limb and predicting a high level of success for someone he has known for a relatively short period of time. He feels more comfortable if he can predict advancement to, perhaps, the next level or to say that the man has average potential. Fortunately, there are some high-potential employees among these young men, and, unfortunately, they are sometimes treated as average.

What the young employee is observed doing has little relationship to what he is expected to do when he becomes a manager. We ask a rater to perform a very difficult task when we ask him to predict how a young man will perform in a managerial assignment while he is observing that man perform the tasks assigned to him in an entry job as an engineer, salesman, or accountant.

People who know the young employee best may be in the least advantageous position to know the requirements for higher level management jobs. Those *above* his immediate supervisor in the organizational hierarchy are probably more familiar with the qualifications required of managers but they are also less closely associated with the employee being evaluated.

These remarks about the problems associated with appraisals of potential of young employees are not meant to imply that we should stop using them. On the contrary, we must continue to use them because we need all of the information we can obtain about employees' qualifications.

There would be no point in discussing the deficiencies of ratings of potential if there were nothing else available to help with this problem. There is.

EARLY RESEARCH

In 1955 Exxon Corporation, at that time Standard Oil Company (New Jersey), began a long-range research program to develop tools and techniques which would help in the identification of employees with management potential. The initial work, referred to as the Early Identification of Management Potential Research Study (EIMP) involved some 500 managers from the parent company and affiliates in the New York area. This study made possible the development of the Personnel Development Series, a battery of tests and questionnaires which has been found to be highly predictive of managerial success.

We will not go into the methodology or the analysis of the data here. However, there is one point which should be made clear. We did use a very empirical approach in establishing the scoring keys for most of the tests and in assigning the weights to be put on each separate test. Success in management was determined by the independent criteria – organization level, salary history, and ratings of effectiveness – not by a psychologist sitting in an armchair and deciding what a manager should look like. Our task was to find out which tests and which items in the tests discriminated between the more successful and the less successful managers and to put them together in a test battery which would measure the extent to which other employees possessed the personal characteristics of those who had been most successful. This we did and we now have this test battery, the Personnel Development Series, available.

Just how closely related the test scores were to success in

management is illustrated in Exhibit 1 on page 84. The criterion here is the overall index of success which is a combination of level in the organization, salary history, and ratings of managerial effectiveness. In this expectancy chart the superior group is defined as those who were in the top third on the overall success criterion. Therefore, the odds of an individual's being in the superior group under past selection and promotion procedures was 33 in 100.

The chart is read as follows: an individual with a weighted test score in the top 20 per cent of the score range has 76 chances in 100 of being in the superior group; one with a score in the next 20 per cent, 47 chances in 100; in the middle 20 per cent, 27 chances; in the next lower 20 per cent, 13 chances; and in the lowest 20 per cent, only 4 chances in 100. The results were substantially the same when we separated the managers by company and by functional activity.

This chart has a couple of important implications. In the first place it demonstrates that there were some individuals who scored high on the tests who were not highly successful managers and that a few were successful in management even though they did not score high on the tests. This situation emphasizes the need to take into consideration *all* the available information about a man when making decisions concerning him. The second implication is that the odds of being successful in management are much better if a man scores high on the tests than if he scores low. This is important if there are limitations on the amount of time and effort that can be expended on management development or if there is a limited number of development assignments available in an organization.

Following the original EIMP study, several North American affiliates carried out field trials on pilot studies of the PDS. In addition, more than 600 employees of Esso Inter-America participated in a major replication of the EIMP study. They included North Americans working in the headquarters at Coral Gables; Latin American employees in Peru, Colombia, and three Central American countries; and North Americans working in Latin America. This was the first attempt to apply the PDS to expatriates and to translate and use the tests in different cultural settings.

All of these studies confirmed the findings of the EIMP study: a substantial relationship existed between the scores on the PDS and the independent criteria of success in the organizations.

In Europe, six studies have been completed to test the applicability of the PDS. Affiliates in which this work was done are those that operate in Denmark, Norway, Holland, Germany, Finland and Belgium.

THE PDS

Before describing the results of the studies which have been completed in Europe, we would like to take a closer look at the PDS and the way it is being used.

What It Measures

One of the most difficult questions to answer about these tests and questionnaires is what they are actually measuring. Operationally one can say that they are measuring personal characteristics which are associated with success in the Exxon organization, but that answer is not too satisfying. Exhibit 2 on page 85 gives some additional information.

There are seven tests in the battery: two tests of mental ability, one a general test and the other a test of non-verbal reasoning; a temperament survey on which the individual describes his own views and attitudes; two personal history inventories which, incidentally, have been our most effective instruments; a description of the way the individual goes about his job; and a test on business orientation. The first four, Series I, can be administered shortly after the man joins the company; the others, Series II, are partly dependent upon experience and can be given after about five years. The right side of the chart outlines some of the characteristics which the PDS measures.

One of the factors is intelligence, a characteristic which is related to managerial success. This is measured not only by the tests of general mental ability but also by items in the background surveys covering such areas as performance in school and college and by the kind of outside activities in which the man participates.

The second factor is the personality makeup of the individual. Included here are his general temperament, the extent to which he has a realistic acceptance of his own ability, and the effectiveness of his personal relationships with other people.

The third factor has to do with the individual's past achievements and the extent to which he has been recognized for them. Included here are achievements in school, early work experiences, and leisure time and community activities.

The fourth major factor is independence and maturity in business situations and in the social environment. The degree of independence and maturity can be assessed in a number of ways over a long period of the man's life.

How It is Used

There is a point which should be emphasized: the PDS is not used for the selection of managers. Rather, it is one means of identifying those employees with the potential to become managers and, as such, provides a new source of information (the employee himself) to supplement the estimates of potential for advancement made by the employee's supervisors. Performance on jobs of increasing difficulty and responsibility represents the real test and, in fact, performance can be thought of as testing the PDS results. To summarize this point, we can say that the implementation of the PDS in an organization does not replace anything we are now doing in management selection and development; the PDS simply provides additional information to assist in decision making. And the executives of the company still make the selections of managers.

There are several specific ways in which managers have found the PDS to be of value:

To uncover promising men earlier so that their development may be aided or accelerated.

To confirm judgements on men whose job performance has been adequately observed so that development may proceed with greater assurance.

To assist in the choice of staff or professional men for tryout as supervisors.

To encourage early administrative review of men whose potential, as viewed both by observed performance and PDS results, appears limited, and who have had an adequate probationary period.

To help analyze whether recruiting efforts are producing an appropriate reservoir of men with management potential.

One of the greatest values of the PDS, related to the first item on the list, is that it gives a company at least five years' lead time on the identification of high-potential employees. Data from one US organization illustrated this point. (Exhibit 3, page 85.) Of the people tested, 281 had scored in the A category (top 8 per cent). The chart shows the potential estimates made by management on these 281 men broken down by the length of service.

The trends apparent in this chart support not only the usefulness of the PDS but also its predictability as to management potential. Even though one accepts the premise that management judgement, over time, is the best evaluator of management potential, it is still clear that the PDS can be effectively utilized as an early predictor of potential and can reduce the time lag required for absolute evaluation. By identifying management potential early in the career, PDS can serve as an effective tool in improving the supply of available talent by moving individuals earlier into positions in which their performance can really be tested. On the other hand, if these same high-potential employees are treated as low potential people and not given an opportunity to show what they can do, there is a good chance that they will begin performing in that manner or leave the company.

This brings us to another value of PDS, that is the capability of identifying young employees whom we definitely do not want to lose until there has been an opportunity to test them on a challenging job assignment. Since the younger and better educated employees do tend to get higher scores on the PDS and since they are also the ones who tend to resign more readily, it is not surprising that more high scorers than low scorers are leaving our European affiliates voluntarily. Nevertheless, it is still discouraging to see so many of the good ones getting away.

Other values of the PDS in personnel development and manpower utilization include the possibilities of making job assignments more in line with employees' capabilities; the stretching of the capacities of those who show promise; and the early elimination from the payroll of those who show no promise, either on the job or on the tests, to make room for more capable people.

EUROPEAN STUDIES

As a first step the tests in the PDS were translated into the appropriate languages. Adaptations to the local cultures were made when necessary, and some items from the background surveys were omitted because of their peculiar North American application. Different verbal reasoning tests were used in Europe because of the difficulties involved in translating the one used in North America.

Two criteria, or independent measures of success in the organization, were common to these studies. These are referred to as the success index and performance evaluation. Independent measures such as these are essential to determine the extent of the relationship between the test scores and success in the organization.

The success index may be thought of as a 'score' which reflects the relative degree of 'success' for each individual in the study in terms of his age, his salary classification, and his company's classification policy. This index is based on the following considerations:

A sound position-classification system takes into account for each job its level of difficulty and, through salary surveys, its value in the larger economic community. Jobs in successively higher level classifications are paid proportionately higher salaries.

An employee promoted to a higher level job must, in the opinion of those making the decision to promote him, have successfully performed his present job and demonstrated the potential to succeed on the higher level job.

A measure of a man's success should take into account his entire career – the many judgements, the many decisions that many supervisors have made about him. The success index does this, and, in so doing, tends to minimize the effects of favorable or unfavorable biases held by one or a few supervisors.

It is assumed that, as a rule, above-average employees will receive promotions more frequently than the average and that below-average employees will receive promotions less frequently if at all.

The success index is, in effect, a measure of level in the organization modified by age. In other words, of two employees of different ages in the same salary group, the younger of the two would have the higher index. Because of the way the index was constructed, it differentiates better for the longer service employees.

The second measure of success, performance evaluation, is based on subjective judgements, typically made by supervisors and managers in the company at levels above those being evaluated. Participants in the study are rated or put in rank order on the basis of their current job performance. An alternation ranking technique is often used, and the ranker is instructed to select the best performer on his list, then the poorest, the next best, the next poorest, and so on. The rankings of each participant on the several ranking lists are combined into an average performance ranking.

In all of our studies we have found that the success index is more closely related to the scores on the PDS than is the performance ranking. There are several reasons for this:

The success index represents an evaluation of a man's career over a long period of time. The performance ranking is based on judgements made at one point in time.

Judgements concerning promotions are more critical to the organization than are those made when ranking on performance and thus receive more care and attention.

The performance ranking calls for evaluation of current performance on present jobs. The tests were designed to predict success in management rather than in sales or staff positions; the assignments held by many of the participants in these studies.

An individual ranked high in a generally poor group could receive a higher score on the overall ranking than one ranked low in a generally good group even though, in absolute terms, the reverse could be true. The computer program used to process the ranking data attempts to correct for this kind of competition, but there is still some distortion.

In spite of the fact that performance evaluation has proved to be a less satisfactory, less reliable, criterion of success, we still find it useful to collect and study both pieces of information and their relationship to the PDS scores. In addition, when we restrict our analysis to those individuals who are consistent on *both* of these criteria, the correlations with the PDS scores are higher than with either of the two studied separately.

More than 90 per cent of those employees invited to participate cooperated in the studies; some of the others were not available at the time of testing but have indicated their willingness to participate at the next opportunity.

The participants in most of these studies were told that the data they provided would be used first for research purposes and that no further use would be made of the test information if the research results were not satisfactory. However, if the studies were successful, the test results would then be reported to the managements of their companies and used as part of the information on which decisions about them would be based. With the exception of the participants in Germany, they were also informed that they would not receive information about their own test results.

Procedure

The general pattern of communications started with a letter from a member of top management announcing the project and inviting employees to participate. Usually group meetings were then held with those invited at which a representative of the Employee Relations Department described the study and the way the results would be used and answered questions about the project. Participation was on a voluntary basis, but, from a realistic viewpoint, we can assume that some employees felt a certain degree of pressure to cooperate.

The tests were administered to the participants in small groups. This required an average of about seven or eight hours for those who took all of the tests, a couple of hours less for the younger employees who took only Series I.

Most of the tests were scored using basically the same scoring keys as those developed in the original EIMP study in the United States. In the Dansk Esso study, the first data to be analyzed, new keys were developed for some of the tests; however, later work demonstrated that this would probably not have been necessary.

Results

The overall results for the total score on the PDS for the European studies were quite consistent with those of the original EIMP study in the US.

The similarity of the findings is even more striking when one examines the relative validity of the different parts of the PDS in the different countries. Although there are some variations from country to country, they are far less than we anticipated when we started this work, and, where the correlations differ from those found in the States, they are just as likely to be higher than lower. Also, as a general rule the most valid of the tests in one country are the same ones that are most valid in others. All of these results can be considered as cross-validation (i.e. broader substantiation) for the original EIMP study.

We were both pleased and surprised with the consistency of these results because they do add to the confidence which can be placed in the PDS. We are not sure that we understand completely the reasons for these findings but we do have some hypotheses which we will check on as we continue our work:

... We were able to sharpen the instruments to a considerable extent by the elimination of parts of the tests which were not effective in discriminating between the more successful and less successful managers, by the revision of many of the items, and by the addition of some new material.

... Those personal characteristics which are related to success which do vary from country to country are not the characteristics which are measured by the PDS. This is quite possible since the PDS accounts for about 50 per cent of the variation in the success criterion leaving the remaining 50 per cent to be accounted for by other characteristics which are not measured by the PDS, as well as a certain amount of 'error variance' in both the PDS and the criterion of success.

... The very nature of a large international industrial organization may overshadow cultural differences between particular countries. This is a plausible explanation since all of the Exxon affiliates are presumably operating under the same general management principles and philosophy and there has been a great deal of cross-fertilization of ideas through management training programs, coordination contacts, and temporary assignments.

... People are people, and we should not have anticipated big differences in the results. There is a great deal of research, both in Exxon and elsewhere, to support this explanation; although people do vary on many surface characteristics, they are quite similar when it comes to basic drives and motives.

There is a rather strong relationship between educational level and PDS scores in Europe; there is also a high correlation between educational level and the success criterion. However, there is still a high correlation between the PDS scores and the criterion even when educational level is held constant. We have also found that combining the test scores with educational level increased substantially the relationship with success beyond that which was possible from a knowledge of educational level alone. In actual practice this issue need not be of great concern since management should look at all available information when making decisions about a man – his education, experience, performance, estimated potential – as well as his test scores. Also, if we can accept the PDS scores as a measure of quality – and the available evidence indicates that we can – we have an additional reason to continue our efforts to upgrade the educational qualifirations of our new employees.

REPORTING AND USING RESULTS

There is no one definition of who is authorized to see the scores, but there are some basic principles which we try to follow:

... In so far as possible, an employee's immediate supervisor will not have knowledge of the test results. The purpose here is to attempt to have the supervisor focus on the man's job performance and evidence which he observes that could be related to the employee's potential for advancement. He should make his judgements about performance and potential independent of the test results.

... The test information should be available at the levels in the organization at which decisions about transfers and promotions are made. Since managers at least one level above the immediate supervisor are typically involved in these decisions, there is no violation of the first principle.

... Test scores will not be reported to management unless the report can include other pertinent information about the individual such as up-to-date ratings on performance and potential, age, service, and salary classification. The purpose of this restriction is to ensure that the manager receiving the information will focus, to the extent possible, on the whole man rather than just that part which is represented by the test scores.

... Test results will not be reported to the individual tested. We have established this principle out of practical considerations rather than because of a fundamental belief that it is proper. We are working with our affiliates in an attempt to develop a practical way of providing information on test performance to individual participants; and in Esso Germany, where employees are receiving feedback of the test scores, the experience is reported to be quite satisfactory.

EXHIBIT 1

EIMP
EXPECTANCY CHART — WEIGHTED TEST SCORE

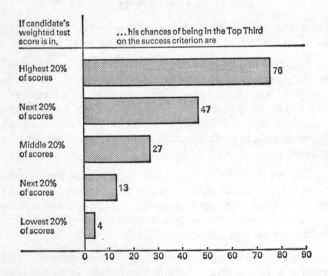

EXHIBIT 2

WHAT THE PDS MEASURES

Tests and Questionnaires	Factors
1. General mental ability	1. Intellectual functioning
2. Analytical reasoning (non-verbal)	2. Emotional functioning — General temperament — Realistic self-perception — Outlook towards interpersonal relations
3. Self-description of attitudes, views, feelings	
4. Personal history inventory (early years)	3. Achievement, recognition, and acceptance in — Scholastic years — Early career — Varied activities
5. Personal history inventory (later years)	
6. Self-description of performance on the job	4. Independence and maturity in — Business situations — Social environment
7. Orientation toward business situations	

EXHIBIT 3

EXTENT TO WHICH HIGH POTENTIAL HAD ALREADY BEEN IDENTIFIED FOR MEN WHO SCORED 'A' ON PDS

Service	Exec. code potential	28 (GP2) potential	Below 28 potential	Potential unknown	Total
10 years and up	37	8	12	0	57
5-9 years — —	28	15	20	4	67
0-4 years — —	18	25	62	52	157
Total — — — —	83	48	94	56	281

CASE STUDY 2

The employee-attitude survey has experienced a renaissance in North America in recent years, due largely to the introduction of the more sophisticated approaches described in Chapter 3. However, managerial resistance to applying survey results, as distinct from authorizing surveys to be made, is by no means rare. What causes this resistance and how it can be managed are the subjects of this paper by Dr David Sirota, who teaches at the Wharton School of Finance and Commerce of the University of Pennsylvania. His consulting work with many companies, notably IBM and Texas Instruments, is the basis of this article.

Why Managers Don't Use Attitude Survey Results

by David Sirota

Edited with permission of the publisher from *Personnel*, January/February 1970. © 1970 by the American Management Association, Inc.

THERE are few large corporations in the United States today that have not, by this time, conducted at least one employee-attitude survey. But despite growing technical sophistication and recognition of the validity of the data collected through questionnaire surveys, there is marked uneasiness on the part of both researchers and managers about this approach. This uneasiness stems from inability or unwillingness to *utilize* survey research findings.

While managers, by and large, eagerly look forward to the results of a survey – and find the initial presentation of the data 'extremely interesting' – the enthusiasm and interest seem almost to disappear within a few weeks. Getting anybody to *do* anything about survey findings becames a Herculean task.

This discussion of some of the major reasons why managers fail to utilize survey research will be based primarily on the author's experiences in one large corporation where, over the last ten years, more than 100 attitude surveys have been conducted, covering tens of thousands of employees.

In terms of data utilization, the results of this company's surveys have been mixed: in some cases considerable action has been taken; in others the findings have had little or no impact. This variability leads to a consideration of the factors that impede or encourage utilization. (Here defined as the degree to which survey results lead to observable changes in the behavior of managers, including modifications initiated by them in company policies and practices for which they are responsible.)

The most influential of these factors seem to be these:

The personal relevance of survey data.

Personal resistance to change.

The role of higher management.

Organizational resistance to change.

Follow-up research.

The role of the researcher.

PERSONAL RELEVANCE

If behavioral change is to be effected, the manager must perceive a relationship between his own behavior and the survey findings. Unless he sees what he has been doing – or not doing – as contributing to the results, he has no reason to think that change on his part is warranted.

This sounds like an obvious statement, but the fact is that survey data are often analyzed and presented in a way that obscures any direct tie-in between a manager's behavior and the results: either the results are analyzed and shown by very broad organizational units, or the presentation is devoted primarily to an analysis and understanding of relationships among abstract variables.

The analysis unit. In many attitude surveys, the data are analyzed only for the *total* organization surveyed. The findings are presented for an entire population – e.g. a plant consisting of many hundreds of employees – with no categorization of the data by subunits within the organization.

Of course, data presented for an entire organization can be useful, especially if they are compared with findings in other organizations. One may learn, for example, that employee attitudes in a plant are significantly poorer than in other plants on certain dimensions, and the discovery of these differences may focus attention on plantwide problems that need correction. However, concentration on broad issues alone has the effect of divesting all managers, except those at the highest levels, of responsibility for initiating corrective action.

When survey data can be broken down into subunits, such as departments, large differences among these units almost always show up. These differences mean that, in addition to company-wide conditions (such as salary policies), there are also forces at work peculiar to individual subunits, such as differences in the way individual managers interpret and administer policies.

Managers assume – and usually rightly – that there is a great deal of this intra-organization variability. They want to know what their own employees are saying. Lacking this information, they do not view the data as being particularly relevant to their own behavior or demanding changes in it.

Intervariable analysis. The analysis of survey data in terms of concrete organization units might be called descriptive analysis, but the data may also be analyzed and presented in terms of relationships among variables, for example, between length of service and job satisfaction, or between method of supervision and attitude toward the manager, or between size of department and attitude toward co-workers.

The generality of the principles derived from intervariable

analysis is both its strength and its weakness. Although these principles help one to understand a wide range of superficially dissimilar phenomena; when the focus is on everybody in general and nobody in particular, the manager can easily avoid confronting the specifics of his own patterns of behavior. What is lacking is a confrontation with evidence about the conceptions that others have of them. Survey data can provide this evidence if they are descriptively analyzed in terms of the particular units for which the managers are responsible. When this is done, intervariable analysis can be helpful to the manager in understanding the data, but these data must be *his*.

An illustration of subunit analysis. In the corporation mentioned earlier, data collected in a survey are now divided by all organizational units. Every manager whose employees participate in the survey receives a report on the attitudes of his own employees. To help preserve anonymity, the only restriction imposed on this procedure is that the manager's unit consist of at least eight employees.

In addition to his own results, the manager receives normative data for comparisons between the attitudes of his employees and those of the total organization of which they are a part. If a previous survey has been conducted in his unit he receives that information too, so that trends over a period of time can be assessed. As a rule, this company's questionnaires contain about 200 items, and a single survey usually includes many hundreds of employees working in dozens of individual departments. Various computer programs have been developed through which the data can be processed quickly and condensed into summary reports for managers.

PERSONAL RESISTANCE TO CHANGE

Thus far we have been concerned primarily with the method of data analysis and presentation, but competence in these areas is no assurance that the information will stimulate behavioral change on the part of the manager who receives it.

Most people resist material in which their behavior is unfavorably evaluated. With few exceptions, the managers who respond in a generally approving, non-defensive manner to survey results are those who 'look good'. But these are the persons for whom little or no behavioral change is indicated.

Defensive reactions to survey data on the part of managers take many forms. The validity of the research instrument may be attacked ('These are all leading questions'), as well as the motives of the researcher ('You're trying to look good by making me look bad'). Various rationalizations will be offered for the negative findings: 'Employees always complain – it's just their nature'; 'The survey was conducted at a bad time'; or, 'One man in the department influenced all the others to answer that way'. Scapegoating can also be anticipated; for example, 'Head-quarters' policies caused all this trouble'.

Some of these reactions may represent a genuine search for explanations, and even arguments that are clearly defensive often contain some elements of truth. It is the pattern of the reactions that is important – the consistent shifting of responsibility for the findings to other persons, things, or events.

Handling resistance. It is important to understand that changing one's behavior on the basis of survey results amounts to an admission of responsibility for these results, that is, an admission of some prior incompetence. For most people, self-esteem is strongly affected by feelings about job competence, and unfavorable survey results bring this competence into question.

There is probably no way to relieve initial defensiveness to any extent. Some managers will exhibit little defensiveness, but this seems to be more a matter of individual personality and position than method of data presentation. Usually, attention to the method of data presentation can help avoid the more extreme manifestations of defensiveness. For example, it is better to show managers data about their own units in private than in group sessions. Still, damping down extreme negative reactions is by no means the same as obviating defensiveness, which is likely to continue as a barrier to utilization of research data no matter what the technique of data presentation.

Given this rather pessimistic assessment and prognosis, it would seem that little in the way of behavioral change can be expected from managers on the basis of survey results. But this is true only if a marked reduction in defensiveness is assumed to be a necessary condition for behavioral change to occur. Actually, while any behavioral change is facilitated by a manager's acceptance of the survey data, it does not depend on it. There are many influences at work in an organization that can be brought to bear to induce change on the part of a manager and indeed the *requirement* to change one's behavior is often a precondition for a reduction in defensiveness. This brings us to a consideration of the key role of higher management in the utilization process.

THE ROLE OF HIGHER MANAGEMENT

It is true that managers react defensively to survey data that negatively affect their feelings of competence, but most managers are continually faced with challenges to their competence, in matters such as department productivity, sales achievement, cost performance, and the like. Whether or not they respond defensively to criticism in these areas is usually of little relevance to higher management, which, if the matter is important, brings to bear the organization's system of sanctions – salary increases, informal recognition, promotions, et cetera – to elicit change.

This, the difference in the degree of change resulting from attitude surveys and that resulting from other measurements, is not accounted for by a difference in defensiveness, but by the difference in the way the measurements are related to the organization's expectations and sanctions. *Little behavioral change on the basis of survey findings can be expected unless managers feel that such change will be rewarded by higher management and its absence will invoke penalties.*

Perhaps this sounds overly harsh, and certainly it is out of keeping with the usual 'human relations' approach that tends to reject or ignore the efficacy of an organization's power structure and of traditional rewards and punishments for achieving behavioral change. But what a manager does is very much a product of these forces. If managers are to take action on survey results they must be convinced that higher management deems it important – not just vaguely desirable – that they do so.

Even if there were no defensiveness, tying research utilization into the system of expectations and sanctions would still be crucial in getting managers to allocate time to it. Few managers can do all the things that, theoretically, they are expected to do, so they must set priorities, and a major determinant in the ordering of these priorities is the attitude of their superiors.

Managers quickly learn to distinguish between the desirable and the really important. In general, work on survey data falls into the former category, and managers find it difficult to resist putting that data aside while they attend to the matters that 'really count'.

A balanced approach. To say that research utilization should be integrated with the system of sanctions is not synonymous with advocating an environment dominated by threat, fear, and coercion. There are reasonable expectations, and there are also reasonable ways to relate sanctions to the fulfillment of these expectations.

In the case of attitude survey utilization, managers will consider higher management's actions reasonable when:

1. The survey data are treated at upper levels as only one of a number of different inputs available regarding the performance of the manager, not as the be-all and end-all in judging his competence.
2. Higher management gives primary emphasis to the future, rather than to the past, that is, has less concern with identifying the 'good guys' and 'bad guys' as measured by the survey than with their effective utilization of the results for improvement.
3. Managers see the data for their units before anybody else.
4. Managers are given sufficient time to study the results and formulate action plans – usually a matter of two or three months.

5. Assistance, if required, is provided to managers in both data interpretation and formulating action plans. This collaboration frequently requires the active involvement of the survey researcher well beyond the initial data-feedback stage.

6. Higher management follows up on progress in the development and implementation of action, with appropriate recognition of those who have paid serious attention to the data and are doing something about it.

ORGANIZATIONAL RESISTANCE

This discussion so far has dealt with individual manager motivation to act on the basis of attitude survey findings. But there are often situations in which a manager's willingness to act is not enough, situations that arise primarily when changes made on the basis of survey data adversely affect others in the organization.

Let's suppose a survey reveals considerable employee dissatisfaction in a manufacturing function, and that the management of this function is genuinely interested in doing something about these findings, studies them thoroughly, and concludes that the dissatisfaction has two major causes. One is the way overtime has been distributed among employees; a check of the records confirms that some employees have been given disproportionate amounts of overtime. Therefore, a more equitable procedure is decided upon and implemented.

This change has little or no effect on anyone outside the manufacturing function, but the second major cause of dissatisfaction seems to be the content of the employees' jobs, which have become so routinized and segmented that they are now devoid of all challenge and interest. In addition to lowered morale, the manufacturing management believes that a severe underutilization of employee skills has resulted.

Resistance by others. A program of job enlargement is launched, but the managers soon run into difficulties. Decisions about methods for enlarging jobs turn out to be the easiest part of the program; it is in getting the approval and cooperation of other areas of the plant that trouble crops up. For example:

1. Job enlargement results in job upgrading, which means higher wage levels, and they, in turn, require the consent of persons such as the controller and wage administrator, whose training and responsibilities are geared to holding expenditures down.
2. There are objections from staff departments such as production control and quality control, whose procedures will have to be modified to mesh effectively with the new structure of enlarged jobs.
3. Managers in other manufacturing functions are disturbed at the prospect of their employees' becoming aware of what is going on and demanding the same changes in their departments.
4. An essentially ideological conflict develops with groups such as industrial engineering, whose training leads them to advocate precisely what the manufacturing managers are trying to eliminate – a high degree of work fractionalization.

The advocates of job enlargement thus find themselves fighting a series of battles that, from a career point of view, may be quite risky for them to undertake. Predictably, under these conditions, the initial enthusiasm for implementing the changes almost always sharply declines and then all but disappears.

This stymying is almost always frowned upon – in theory – as an unfavorable feature of organizational life, impeding 'progress', but it can also be argued that such conflict is the organization's system of checks-and-balances and as such helps to assure a 'trial' for ideas before they are implemented. The flaw in this reasoning is not that there is a 'trial', but that quite often the trial is not fair, because of power inequality of the opposing parties.

Conflict resolution. Equalizing the sides takes the influence of higher management, and in the case of proposals based on survey results, this intervention would have two major components:

First, it involves continuing and heavy emphasis by higher

management on its concern that corrective action be taken. Second, higher management's influence must be brought to bear to stimulate direct interaction between managers initiating the changes and those likely to be affected by them. Ideally, these sessions would be open exchanges of views, with the goal of arriving at mutually agreeable action plans, and this is not so difficult as one might suppose.

FOLLOW-UP RESEARCH

Surveys are usually conducted in companies to measure employee attitudes at a particular time. Somebody decides that it would be wise to find out 'what our employees are thinking', a survey is administered, the data are studied, then, if all goes as planned, action plans are formulated and implemented. The program ends there, although perhaps, years later, it is felt that 'we had better find out what our employees are thinking *now*', and so another survey is conducted.

While data collected through any one survey can yield valuable information for organizational improvement, the usefulness of the technique is greatly enhanced when it is carried out on a periodic and regular basis, so that the effectiveness of the action taken can be assessed systematically.

A follow-up survey (in which questions are worded essentially like those in the earlier study) sometimes reveals that the steps taken have not significantly alleviated the problems of a unit, and in this case, management will have to reconsider what has been done and formulate new plans.

More often, however, re-surveys show that action taken after serious consideration of the earlier survey's findings has resulted in at least some improvement. Still, the improvement may be uneven, occurring in certain attitude dimensions but not others, or among certain categories of employees but not others. By examining these new data thoroughly, in conjunction with an equally thorough retrospective analysis of exactly what actions have been taken, the managers can learn a great deal about the conditions that affect change processes. For example, they may learn that job enlargement results in favorable change only when it is accompanied by careful training of employees in the new work methods, or by job level and salary improvements.

What this adds up to is that taking action on the basis of survey results should be viewed in dynamic terms: it is a process taking place over a time in which there is as much interplay as possible between behavioral change and feedback as to results.

THE ROLE OF THE RESEARCHER

Having considered the line manager and obstacles to his research utilization, now we should consider the role of the researcher beyond his responsibilities for data analysis and feedback.

Recommending action. Many managements believe that the researcher's job includes making recommendations for corrective action after the survey data are in, because he knows the data best, his training in the behavioral sciences gives him special insight into organizational problems and methods for correcting them, and he is 'objective'.

It is really more likely, however, that having the researcher make action recommendations acts as an impediment, rather than an aid, to effective utilization of the survey findings, for two major reasons.

First, researchers as a rule simply do not know enough to make meaningful recommendations. The usefulness and success of most action recommendations depend on thorough knowledge not only of the data, but also of the business, technological, and organizational environments of the group surveyed.

For example, it does not make much sense to recommend a change in the salary level of a group without taking into account the effect of this change on the company's total salary structure; or to recommend decentralization of authority (based on complaints about 'overcontrol') without having considered the company's needs for coordination; or to recommend increased manpower without knowledge of employee productivity, training costs, anticipated product developments, and so forth.

In most circumstances it is unrealistic to expect one man, or even a team of researchers, to have this detailed information about a company. Because they do not have it, researchers are prone to make recommendations that are often disappointing to management – either trivial ('more notices about recreational activities on the bulletin board') or meaninglessly general ('more emphasis on good human relations practices when dealing with employees').

Neither of these kinds of recommendation is truly helpful, and the trivial ones are actually a disservice, because, although they can be quickly and easily implemented, they give the illusion of 'action' on the basis of survey findings while the more serious problems the survey may have uncovered go unattended.

A second disadvantage in making the researcher responsible for recommending changes is that this delegation weakens the motivation of managers to make the changes work. In general, people are much more committed to assuring the success of plans that they themselves have formulated than of those recommended to them by others.

Perhaps in some instances the researcher can develop a change program that, at least on paper, holds great promise of improvement, but it is the managers who are going to have to implement the program, and, since it is somebody else's program, they have little to lose if it fails and little to gain if it works.

Helping others change. Does this mean that the researcher bows out entirely once he presents and interprets his data, reappearing only to conduct the evaluative re-survey? Not at all; once his findings are analyzed and reported, the researcher's responsibility is to help create a setting in which effective action can be generated. That is, he shifts from the pure research role to one in which his social-psychological skills and knowledge are applied in helping managers both in formulating plans and in working together productively.

This is a complex role, with these facets:

1. Serving as a sounding board for the managers' ideas as they study the data.
2. Bringing past research and theory to bear on their problems.
3. Carrying out various analyses of their data for them and suggesting ways of collecting additional data, such as in-depth interviews with employees.
4. Suggesting meetings with others in the organization grappling with the same problems and with those likely to be affected by the solutions to these problems.
5. Working in these meetings to facilitate openness in the exchange of ideas and in dealing with conflict.
6. Helping to assure frequent contact and exchange of opinions with higher management as action plans develop.

A great deal of attitude survey work in industry falls short of its promise or potential because management sees the researcher's task as essentially completed once he presents his results – the conclusion of 'recommendations' really acts to close the matter. But this is a serious underutilization of the skills of most researchers in this field; their experience and knowledge in helping managers translate statistics into action are among the major contributions they can make.

CASE STUDY 3

This paper was written by Mr Burden as a report of his experiences as a department manager at a refinery of Shell Oil Company in England. Although he calls his approach 'participative', and it clearly was that, many of the changes he introduced would also fit quite appropriately under the heading of job enrichment. The results he obtained are similar to those reported in other settings and are presented here both for their inherent interest and as an example of successful application of behavioral science principles by a British organization. An edited version of this paper is reproduced here by courtesy of Shell UK Ltd.

A Participative Approach to Management

by D. W. E. Burden

IN the summer of 1965, the oil manufacturing function of Shell in the UK, with the assistance of the Tavistock Institute of Human Relations, set out to define its overall objectives and the underlying management philosophy against which they were to be achieved.

The philosophy was written down and it was contended that the business and social objectives of the company could best be achieved through use of the socio-technical concept of organization. This states that any organization is made up of a technical system of plant and equipment, and a social system of people and their organization. The best results are achieved by considering the two systems together in a complementary supportive manner to achieve their joint-optimization – less, possibly, than the optimum of either system viewed in isolation but the 'best-fit' of the two together.

Early in 1966 I was asked to take over as Department Manager of the Micro-Wax Department in Shell's Stanlow Refinery at Ellesmere Port in Cheshire.

During 1965 and 1966 some forty conferences were held involving refinery personnel from Senior Management to first-line Supervision to discuss the philosophy and objectives-statement. By spring 1966 the management climate in the refinery was such that new ideas and new methods, particularly in relation to the social system were more readily accepted. This supportive management climate is most important if any attempts to innovate are to succeed, because it allows risk-taking without which most management ideas are still-born.

What did I find in spring 1966 when I became Manager of Micro-Wax Department? Looking first at the technical system I found that for about a year the plant had been through a series of serious difficulties which appeared to stem from the enforced change to a different feed material from that for which the plant was designed. Pressure from the market had demanded continued operation of parts of the plant which were in need of overhaul and hence operating at less than maximum efficiency. This had resulted of course in lowered output, more pressure from the market, less time still for maintenance and so on – producing the inevitable spiral towards complete shutdown. Technical help was available of course, but the main problems were short-term practical operating ones.

What about the social system? Morale amongst the plant operators was low. They had very little confidence in the equipment they controlled. Because of the extremely serious market position the previous manager had issued instructions that no alterations were to be made to plant operating conditions without his permission. This loss of control by those actually operating the plant led to some loss in their commitment. They had ideas on how matters might be improved but were not allowed to test them without reference to higher authority. As a result few of these ideas were suggested.

The plant supervisors were frustrated – not only by repeated mechanical breakdown of the plant and consequent long hours of work but primarily because they were not able to change the method of working either. What had to be done now was to inject a will to win into the operators and supervision. I saw this being achieved by involving them fully in determining the plan to recover from the serious situation which confronted us.

The first departmental meeting was held in the Manager's office with the plant Senior Operator, foreman and supervisor present. The Senior Operator was asked to hold a meeting with his shift team to pass on information obtained from the departmental meeting. The meeting examined many of the difficulties put forward by foremen, supervisor and Senior Operator. A meeting was held every week, and gradually as the short-term problems of the plant were solved more general topics relating to the operation of the department were discussed.

The meeting was later moved to the plant mess-room where all the operators were able to attend – the supervisors took turns in keeping a watching brief on the plant. This expanded meeting provided the opportunity for joint problem-solving rather than the indirect participation of the earlier meetings in which members had to be limited.

It is worth noting that it was about a year after the venue was moved to the mess-room before complete freedom of expression became apparent amongst the operators. So it was more than two years after positive steps had been taken to involve operators in the running of the department before the atmosphere was fully participative. And this in a management climate which was favorable. I highlight this to give some idea of the time-lag involved in attitude and consequent behavior change – we are not dealing in the short term.

The establishment of the weekly departmental meeting as an integral part of the process of managing the plant was the initial step in the growth of a participative style of management within the department. Over the two years following this first step a number of changes were introduced.

Because of the layout and design of the plant, it was possible to organize jobs so that each operator had a complete unit to control – including the instrument panel for that unit which was in the main plant control-room. This fulfilled the psychological need which men have to do a job which is complete in itself. It also made possible a high degree of job flexibility. Each operator was encouraged to learn each of the four main process units so that maximum advantage could be derived from this opportunity for flexibility. Because the operators became experienced in operating the different types of unit in the plant they were good candidates for promotion to more senior positions on other plants in the refinery.

Operators experienced on one unit and now operating another unit on the plant were always willing to help less experienced operators during minor unit upsets. This feeling of competent back-up allowed training to continue even though the shift team did not have a fully flexible crew. This side of flexibility – work-sharing to help colleagues out of temporary difficulties – was a most important facet. Without it job training and consequent promotion would not have been possible at anything like the rate achieved.

Flexibility within a shift is one thing – flexibility across shift teams is another. There tends to be strong identification with a particular shift. So much so in fact that even upon promotion or job change shift-workers will often ask to stay on the same shift. The reasons for this of course are not difficult to find. The group of shift-teams becomes a strong social group. They organize dances and sports activities together and probably most important of all often share transport to and from work. So to ask for flexibility between shifts one is attempting to change the well-established social order – albeit only temporarily.

In order to allow free movement between shifts as required for training and sickness cover the Senior Operators of each shift were given the authority to cover as they thought necessary. In order to facilitate this movement clocking was abolished, and the Senior Operators given the responsibility of recording absence. The presence of the time-clock was seen not only as a deterrent to inter-shift flexibility but also as a lack of trust in the operators. Shift work is itself a regulator: clocks are not necessary.

This one move opened up many possibilities for the operators, and they took full advantage of them. The absence of the clock meant that they could come and go to some extent to suit their own social lives providing they planned ahead and arranged relief cover with their Senior Operator's approval. (This approval was given providing the replacement operator was competent and continued safe operation of the plant was assured.) This was done frequently and far from causing problems of administration it became a fully self-regulating system. Only if agreement could not be reached would the foreman arbitrate – and he did this very rarely.

The sickness/absence figure for the plant fell steadily through 1966, 1967 and 1968 and although it is not possible to pinpoint the reason, it is felt that with a cover system of the type adopted, absence became a more personal thing – one knew who was being inconvenienced – and this had something to do with this fall.

Another of the changes made concerned the operating log. Often continuous process work operators are expected to fill in record sheets concerning process conditions at set intervals of time. They often do not know why they record this information nor to what use it is put. An operating log sheet for the plant was designed in consultation with the operators. One major feature of this log sheet – in fact sheets because it was decided to keep one for each unit and a master balance sheet – was that records were required only every four hours – and then only on pre-determined vital instruments. The emphasis was moved from the mechanical act of putting figures on paper, to that of ensuring that the instruments functioned properly and were quickly rectified if they did not. The whole exercise of keeping information now had a purpose, seen and understood by the operators, and what is most important they could determine for themselves the results of their efforts.

To have information about the performance of the plant is one thing – to use it, another. The Senior Operators had the authority to make alterations to plant conditions in order to meet the program. This program, determined daily by the supervisor against the plan discussed at the weekly meetings, was outlined to the Senior Operators. The program was deliberately drawn up to enable the Senior Operators to exercise judgement, and they had the authority to exercise judgement.

The process of change from an authoritarian system towards a participative one was most interesting to observe. For several months after the Senior Operator's authority to alter plant conditions was agreed the Department Manager and other members of the supervisory staff were telephoned out of day-work hours to discuss problems as seen by the Senior Operators. This was a most critical period because, again with hindsight, this was the period in which the Senior Operators were adjusting to the new way of working. Invariably the telephone call was to confirm that action proposed was correct although it was often not phrased that way – often the problem itself was stated and the analysis of the situation already done by the Senior Operator had to be drawn from him. Refusal by the day staff to do any more than ask questions and prompt answers at this stage is now seen as a very important part of the development of the Senior Operators. They gradually learned to use their skills and to seek assurance only when they really needed it. The telephone calls became routine reports of the state of the plant at the end of the shift. It was probably six months or so before this state of affairs was reached.

Of course some mistakes were made – but these were used to improve knowledge rather than as disciplinary matters. Trust is a very important part of true delegation. I think we were demonstrating that given responsibility and the requisite authority our Senior Operators were perfectly capable of running the plant safely and efficiently – several million pounds' worth of equipment.

In order to make the fullest use of their knowledge and to help remove frustration the Senior Supervisor and Day Foreman were encouraged to produce ideas for improvements to the plant. As a general principle plans of any proposed alteration to the plant were left in the main plant control-room for all the operators to see and to comment upon.

An interesting example of this type of work is the re-designed routing of the pipelines which carry liquid wax between various plant storage tanks. The foreman and supervisor complained bitterly about the poor design of the pipeline routes and the product waste caused because of complicated flushing-out procedures. They were asked to design a better scheme. This is the method they used. They first wrote down a list of all the transfers normally carried out, and then a list of desirable transfers which the present system would not allow. Then these lists were given to the shift operators for them to study and enlarge if possible. Some alterations and additions were made. Then with knowledge of the total transfer scheme required a sketch of a linework system which made it possible was drawn.

The estimate of £500 was accepted. The plant Day Foreman then drew up a construction plan which allowed work to be done whilst the plant was still running and he then supervised the work through to completion. As a result of the modifications the flushing-out operations were considerably reduced and in fact the savings in re-processing costs paid for the modifications in less than a month. To give some idea of the magnitude of the re-routing task – there are fifty-six storage tanks involved, each with at least two lines, and the whole system is inter-connected via four transfer pumps. By a series of quite ingenious small cross-connections the whole system was made much more flexible. So carefully was the scheme planned that far from using more valves to isolate one part of the system from another, they used the existing valves – and had two spare ones at the end.

A second example of the change in the jobs of supervision occurred in the financial sphere. The Senior Supervisor and Day Foreman were involved with the Department Manager in producing the operating budget and once the allocation of funds for their particular spheres of responsibility had been determined they were given complete discretion over the expenditure, with no control by the Department Manager – other than the commitment not to exceed the agreed budget figures.

In order to evaluate certain parts of the plant for various reasons, test runs are arranged from time to time. For successful evaluation, it is essential that plant conditions remain as steady as possible and that samples and readings are taken carefully and at the prescribed times. The refinery practice has been for the technologist responsible for the test run to arrange for sample containers to be provided from the laboratory and then to take the samples himself. The argument has been that since the samples are to undergo careful analysis to be used in extensive calculations it is vital to have properly taken samples. In other words – one cannot trust plant operators to take samples properly.

What we did – in consultation with the technologist involved and the operators was to provide, with a short note from the technologist, information on the object of the test run. The need for accuracy was stressed – and the rest, accurate recording of information, careful taking of samples, steady operation of the plant was left to the operators. They were of course much more involved in the whole process and very interested in its successful outcome. When completed, a copy of the test run report was left in the control-room for the operators to read. It is interesting to note that these reports were the source of many questions by the operators on plant operation, and one suggestion made as a result of test run data by a plant operator produced a plant modification which enabled the plant to continue running a few months later when it would otherwise have shut down.

We examined the way in which samples were drawn for testing. Again this is normally done against a set time schedule, in order that laboratory work may be scheduled. The disadvantage of this system is that it does not take account of the variations in plant conditions and as a consequence the laboratory results do not provide the sure guide to quality that one would hope for. There is also a considerable time-lag in a large refinery in transporting the samples to the laboratory. An operator who takes samples at specified times is not encouraged to be involved with the result – and the time-lag means that in any case the result is often not available until the end of his shift.

To overcome both the time-lag and encourage operator involvement it was suggested that the operators might do much of their own testing on the plant. The rigid testing schedule was withdrawn and operators were asked to test when they felt it necessary in order to make on-grade product. We found that during normal operation much less testing was done – but under abnormal circumstances much more testing was done. As a result doubtful material, which previously had run to off-grade storage until the laboratory results were available, was now checked frequently and put to on-grade storage much sooner, thus reducing the amount of re-processing required. The financial savings were not great although occasionally £100 re-processing costs would be saved in a shift.

A scheme was devised by Accounts Department whereby tank stocks were to be recorded on a form used directly as a source document for the computer. When this was first proposed to Wax Department, the operator controlling the tanks was asked to come to the Department Manager's office and join in the discussions with the Computer personnel. After examining the proposal form and listening to an explanation of how the proposed system would work the operator suggested replacing our existing record form completely with the new form – and simply using a copy for plant records. This suggestion was welcomed and an explanation of the system was given to all the operators controlling plant storage tanks. The effectiveness of this example of direct involvement is demonstrated by the fact that difficulties were experienced in some other departments in the refinery with computerized documentation of tank stocks, whilst in the Micro-Wax Plant the new system had a trouble-free introduction.

All these examples together make up the history of a participative approach to the management of the Micro-Wax Department. Ideally, of course, it would be nice to have a clean experimental situation with 'before' and 'after' measures. These are not available because the work described was done as part of an on-going management process and not as an experimental project to test a management technique. Indeed it is claimed that such an approach will inevitably fail if it is looked upon merely as a technique. Participation is an attitude of mind and a mode of management behavior and stems from a concern for, and desire to, develop human ability.

It is over a year now since the author left the plant and in that time the new Departmental Manager has increased still further the authority and responsibility of the department supervision to the point where they are now virtually running the department. Recently it was decided to purchase some new equipment for the plant – one piece to cost approximately £100,000. The foreman and supervisor between them drew up the operating specification required, entertained visiting technical representatives, and after showing them the plant discussed their plans with them. Finally they made the selection and it is the operating Day Foreman who will liaise with the manufacturers during construction.

This article might have been headed 'How to do Yourself Out of a Job' – but if liberating the latent talents of others leads in this direction, as it is bound to do, then we must recognize it. It implies more effective manpower planning – we pay a great deal of attention to financial and technical planning (the 'technical system'), but generally not enough to 'social system' planning. It is easier in an expanding environment, as the one discussed was of course; but it is just as important in a static or even contracting environment to make effective use of the human resources – to plan them properly. Certainly the period discussed was at times a stressful one for the Departmental Manager, and very hard work – but if you derive satisfaction from watching other people grow then the stress and the hard work is well worthwhile.

CASE STUDY 4

Job enrichment has a tendency to change the manager's
role more than those of their subordinates whose jobs
were the focus of the enrichment. This is only one of several
obstacles to the effective implementation of this method. At
present, job enrichment and related methods are receiving
considerable attention, chiefly because of their potential
impact on productivity. However, this interest must be
tempered with a realistic appreciation of the difficulties
that are likely to be encountered in actual practice. Job
enrichment is, after all, an *intervention* in an existing
system, and as such is likely to encounter the typical mis-
understandings; lack of attention and enthusiasm and
outright resistance that greet all interventions – at least
initially.

Dr Sirota, the senior author of the paper that follows,
has already been introduced as the author of Case Study 2.
Mr Wolfson is a consultant in New York City. In this
article they discuss their experiences in implementing job
enrichment programs, and some of the resistances they
have encountered.

Job Enrichment: What Are the Obstacles?

by David Sirota and Alan D. Wolfson

Edited with permission of the publisher from *Personnel*, May/
June 1972. © 1972 by the American Management Association,
Inc.

JOB enrichment may be defined as the redesign of a job to provide a worker with greater responsibility, more autonomy in carrying out that responsibility, closure (a complete job), and more timely feedback about his performance. Over the past half-dozen years or so, there has been a great deal of publicity and propaganda about job enrichment – primarily from Frederick Herzberg and his followers – and it is likely that most American managers have by now had at least some exposure to the concept and that many have been favorably impressed by it.

It is not easy to dismiss the very considerable evidence demonstrating the significant morale and performance benefits of enrichment. Yet, despite the widespread knowledge about it and public acknowledgement of its usefulness, its application to actual modification of jobs in organizations has been disappointing. The concept still gets its greatest play in the management development classroom, but the enthusiasm generated there often seems to be almost entirely dissipated when the managers return to their jobs.

As with so many fundamental changes, there are enormous obstacles to translating acceptance of job enrichment into a visible and significant behavioral effect. The conversion of job enrichment concepts into actual job changes is much more difficult than might at first be imagined.

Proponents of job enrichment also stress that the use of enrichment will increase the effectiveness, as well as the happiness, of workers. Very impressive evidence has been presented to support these claims, the most noteworthy of which comes from studies in the American Telephone and Telegraph Company, where Robert Ford and his associates have been engaged in intensive job enrichment work. They report all but one of their projects as being successful.

Almost all of that AT&T work has been done on white-collar jobs. Some critics of job enrichment argue that its application is appropriate primarily for these and for professional and managerial employees, because most blue-collar workers are interested solely in money, and, even if they do have other goals, such as job challenge, it would be extremely difficult to change most blue-collar jobs without large economic costs. This view is pretty well refuted, however, by the experiences in manufacturing operations of corporations such as Maytag, Motorola, and Non Linear Systems. In all these firms, marked improvements in quality and productivity have been achieved by converting traditional, fragmented assembly lines into operations that allow employees to complete entire assemblies. Non Linear Systems has gone a step further than the others in encouraging employees, after dividing them into work teams, to get involved in decisions normally reserved to management about production methods, division of labor, and work pace.

It therefore seems clear that job enrichment need not be limited to the white-collar work force – that, although the nature of factory workers and factory technology appears to be a severe constraint, the fact is that here, as well as in the office, significant job enrichment has been effected and major performance improvements have been achieved.

THE UTILIZATION OF PEOPLE

In our work, we have found it useful to think about job enrichment in terms of manpower utilization. Most managements are keenly aware of the widespread and serious underutilization of people in industry. The traditional view of utilization – that one that, for example, guides the work of many industrial engineers – boils down to the quantitative one of keeping people busy, and, of course, companies do suffer from employees simply not having enough work to do. But the real loss is not a quantitative matter at all; rather, it is the underutilization of the skills and abilities of workers. We hire human beings with considerable talent and considerable ambition, but for many of them we have created jobs appropriate to robots. The man who spends his day tightening nuts on the assembly line goes home at night to dismantle and rebuild an automobile engine; the staff man who finds his working hours consumed by paperwork and trivia goes home at night to serve on the board of education of his community.

Underutilization may be thought of as having two facets, motivational and rational:

Motivational – the underutilization of energy. Because of the inherent triviality and boredom of many jobs, their occupants become almost totally unmotivated to perform them well and, indeed, sometimes are actually motivated to perform them poorly.

Rational – the underutilization of skills and abilities. It is clear that anybody who can take apart and put together an automobile engine can do more than turn nuts on an assembly line, but, it might be argued, *somebody* has to turn those nuts – that's the job. However, it is precisely the contention of job enrichment practitioners that, in fact, that does not have to be the job, that work can be redesigned to utilize the talents of a company's workforce much more fully.

With good will, good sense, and considerable verbal acceptance on the side of job enrichment, why hasn't it been more widely adopted? The reasons, as we see them, fall into eleven basic categories:

1. *Educational.* In traditional management development, managers are bombarded by theory and simulated applications, with the assumption – or hope – that something positive will happen when the managers return to their work environments. But it is a great deal easier to preach concepts such as delegation and closure than to translate these job enrichment principles into specific changes in work content. The fact is that managers often don't know how to go about it, and their lack of procedural knowledge and skill, plus some false starts, can quickly wither continued interest.

2. *Ideological.* The belief that job fragmentation and rigid controls over workers are necessary for productive efficiency still prevails in most companies, not just among industrial engineers, but among line managers as well. Thus, the manager wanting to engage in job enrichment may find himself, at best, ignored by

many of his peers and his own management, and, at worst, instructed to stop his efforts.

Related problems derive from the perception of job enrichment as another human relations 'happiness' program. Because job enrichment concerns people and is meant to increase the satisfaction of these people, and because it is often initiated by personnel or management development specialists, it comes to be viewed as something akin to an additional employee benefit.

3. *Organizational.* There are three aspects to be considered here. First, job enrichment is an investment, a current cost incurred for future return. But organizational pressures are such that the major concerns of managers tend to be short-run in nature – getting the work out *today*, with much less interest in whether it can be done better tomorrow.

Second, organizations are dynamic, with workers and managers changing jobs often, and the shorter the time a manager expects to be in a job, the less interest he has in projects oriented toward the future. Also, job enrichment projects are begun and then discontinued as new managers, not involved from the beginning, take over.

Finally, there are the obstacles that derive from the functional form of organizations, particularly from the vested interests of functions. Some of the changes resulting from job enrichment necessitate taking work from one function in the company and giving it to another. For example, enriching the jobs of machine operators often involves giving them some maintenance responsibilities, and it is not always easy to enlist the support and co-operation of the maintenance people in this switch.

4. *Managerial.* Roadblocks to job enrichment may also be created by the manager himself and the way he views his environment. In the first place, he may be activated by a general resistance to change. For example:

– As long as a manager continues to do things the way they have always been done, he is safer when something goes wrong. Change carries the threat that the blame for subsequent difficulties will be put on the shoulders of the innovator, whether or not they were due to his actions.

– Change often represents an implicit admission that the past behavior has been in error; for many managers, it is akin to eating crow.

– Change may bring new and unfamiliar conditions in which the manager senses ahead of time that he might feel uncomfortable and inadequate.

These reasons for managers' resisting change are reinforced by aspects of job enrichment peculiar to it. First, there is the perceived loss of control as responsibilities are placed in the hands of workers. One that is especially likely to arouse anxiety is the reduction in traditional quality control audits as workers are made responsible for their own quality. Then, too, there is the manager's fear that through job enrichment, he will wind up with little or no work to do. One of the most fertile sources of enrichment for subordinates is the work done by their bosses, much of which either is unnecessary (for example, the time he spends monitoring his people) or can be pushed down to his employees (such as decisions about detailed work methods).

It takes most managers some time to recognize that the delegation of activities to their subordinates gives them the opportunity to get into true management, such as long-range planning.

5. *Technological.* Because there are real and encompassing constraints imposed by the technology with which work is done, the changes that ideally should be made in jobs would often (especially in manufacturing operations) require considerable investment in new equipment or facilities. Unfortunately, job enrichment is still seen by most managements as too 'iffy' a proposition to warrant large-scale expenditures on its behalf. And there is not much that the enrichment practitioner can do about it.

But there is another side to this obstacle about which a great deal can be done – the belief that technology makes *any* change impossible for large classes of jobs or, if possible, perforce trivial. The Maytag, Motorola and Non Linear Systems experiences refute this belief, proving that even within the limitations of assembly line technology significant modifications in work can be made. It is the demonstration of the *feasibility* of enrichment that is among the first tasks of the enrichment practitioner.

6. *The employee.* As with technology, we have here both real and imagined constraints. Sometimes employees are either incapable of doing enriched jobs or unwilling to do them. In no way does job enrichment compensate for incompetence, and it is not going to alter a deeply ingrained fear or dislike of responsibility, either. Obviously, then, job changes need to be tailored to individual capabilities and motivations, and, indeed, sometimes the situation calls for 'de-enrichment' of jobs.

Our experience has shown, however, that the overwhelming majority of employees are both able and eager to handle greatly increased responsibility. The real trouble is managers' refusal to recognize that this is so, and here we see an aspect of the ideological issue discussed earlier. The belief in strong controls and fragmented work derives, in part, from a rather pessimistic view of workers' potential and motivation.

7. *The enricher.* When the job enrichment practitioner is unsuccessful in his effort, he is often inclined to knock the client as 'backward looking', 'unimaginative', or 'scared', instead of taking a hard look at himself and his methods. If he did, he might find that a good deal of the fault is his.

As is true of many new and attractive ideas, in job enrichment a quasi-religious flavor and fervor have grown up, and a set of prescribed rituals has emerged that the faithful must follow. For example, thou shalt use greenlighting (a brainstorming technique for developing enrichment ideas), and thou shalt not involve employees in the enriching process. Perhaps dogmatism and doctrinal purity are necessary in the early stages of a movement devoted to such far-reaching reforms.

But it should be pointed out that much of the rigidity is not to be taken too solemnly. There are many paths to effective job enrichment, as is evidenced by the apparently equal success of diverse approaches used in various companies. For example, the procedure at AT&T is not to involve employees in the generation of ideas about how their jobs could be enriched, and AT&T has been successful with this approach. At Texas Instruments, on the other hand, the employees are heavily involved in idea-generation, and this company, too, has been successful. The true believers deny the value of organization development efforts in conjunction with job enrichment, but Western Union has achieved a great deal with this kind of integration.

The professional journals are filled with controversy about Herzberg's theory; these academic disputes need not concern the manager, but, in practical context, Herzberg's followers are so enamored of his theory that experienced managers often find it difficult to take them seriously. These managers know that it would be folly to forget for one moment that their employees are also working for a living. Managers have seen financial incentives in operation and know that they can and do have a very considerable influence on employee motivation and productivity. And they have also seen how economic insecurity can motivate workers to resist productivity improvements. Finally, they know of the dangers inherent in a philosophy that doesn't insist on commensurate pay increases when responsibility levels are raised.

8. *Diagnosis.* Related to the rigidity of many enrichment practitioners is the glaring lack of systematic diagnosis in many of the organizations in which this work is done. Job enrichment is passing through a faddish phase, and one of the characteristics of a solution-in-vogue is that it tends to be recommended for *all* ailments, and even when there are none. (The T-Group, management-by-objectives, Managerial Grid, and so forth have all passed through similar phases.) While proper diagnosis to determine whether work content is indeed a problem may be distasteful to the zealous practitioner eager to sell his services, its absence almost invariably works to everyone's disadvantage.

If, say, a company's problem is really interpersonal in nature, organizational development techniques would be a more appropriate recommendation. Changing work content would not only do nothing to alleviate the situation; it could actually aggravate the problem, because, in general, the more enriched a job, the greater the complexity of interpersonal relationships in which the employee has to engage, and therefore the more important that these relationships be satisfactory. Hence, there is a critical need for competent diagnosis before job enrichment is undertaken.

9. '*Prove it here*.' There is a strong tendency among managers to stress the uniqueness of their own organizations, whether they be companies, plants within a company, or departments within a plant. Of course, like no two persons, no two organizations are identical, but unique is a widely abused word. Differences are seldom as large or as important as people pretend them to be, but when it comes to activities like job enrichment, many managers believe the differences are definitive; very few are willing to accept AT&T's experiences as 'proof' that job enrichment will work in their own organizations, so its validity has to be proved all over again.

10. '*Nothing new here*.' In a sense, opposite to the 'prove it here' problem is the reaction of managers that there is really nothing much to prove. Job enrichment is 'just good management', and 'We've being doing it for years. (Where we haven't been doing it, it is for good reasons, such as technology.)' This is one of the most difficult of all barriers to overcome, because the opponent claims he's really on your side.

11. *Time*. We come, finally, to the manager's investment of his own time in his work. Rare, indeed, is the job enrichment project that does not require many weeks for planning, idea development, and actual implementation of job changes. Some managers who enter this activity wholeheartedly find their enthusiasm gradually drained by the time it consumes. Thus, time is a barrier not necessarily to getting the process started, but rather to keeping it going.

The discussion of the foregoing eleven points pretty well

summarizes the many obstacles we have encountered in two years of job enrichment work. At this point, even those most convinced of the need for job enrichment might be ready to throw in the towel, but forewarned is forearmed, and the intent in going over all the caveats was simply to emphasize the need for introducing this activity properly.

CASE STUDY 5

The organization development movement is similar to job enrichment in that both represent interventions in on-going systems. In the case of organization development, the intervention is in human relationships, with the intent of helping individuals and groups to contribute to, rather than detract from, each other's effectiveness. A very wide variety of activities has developed under this general heading, and it is regrettably true that much of this has produced little but momentary titillation. But if we sift out such unfortunate aberrations there remain methods with substantial accomplishments to their credit. One of these is 'team building', which is essentially a controlled or managed variation of sensitivity training.

The following paper by Sheldon Davis is a description of his company's experiences with this approach to organization development. Mr Davis is Vice-President for industrial relations of TRW Systems, Inc. This is an edited version of an article that originally appeared in a magazine that has since ceased publication.

Building More Effective Teams

by Sheldon A. Davis

Edited from an article originally published in *Innovation* Magazine, October 1970. Reprinted by permission of Trustee in Bankruptcy for Technology Communication, Inc.

119

A FEW years ago, in the course of my industrial relations work here at TRW Systems, I asked one of our managers of manufacturing if he could see any differences between the ways the two major project managers he was doing work for interacted with him.

'Whenever I have a problem with my counterpart in the first project office,' he said, 'it immediately gets escalated. If he doesn't like something that's going on he goes to his boss who, in turn, mobilizes his boss – a vice-president. Then that vice-president goes over to the vice-president of manufacturing, and the problem comes down that chain, and there's a big meeting. After a couple of hours of wrangling, we might get to the heart of the problem and resolve it in a bloody kind of way.

'Whenever a problem arises with the other group, my counterpart and I get together, and work it out in ten minutes or so. The problems are about the same. In the one case, though, we have this escalation and blood-bath cycle, while in the other one we have short meetings and almost nothing has to be escalated.'

As soon as the manufacturing manager had described the contrasting situations, I knew what the answer was. The two project teams were different from one another in a crucial way:

The men in the second group had spent considerable time and effort in trying to understand how they functioned as a unit and, in particular, how they functioned in their relations with manufacturing.

By contrast, the first group had paid little or no attention to the interpersonal aspects of their work, and were paying a stiff price for not having done so.

The first project manager, you see, was making certain assumptions about the manufacturing manager. Something like this: 'If I don't go all the way upstairs and raise hell, we'll never resolve our problems. The manufacturing guy doesn't really care about our project; he's just another one of those manufacturing types who can't understand the sophisticated engineering we're doing.'

The second project manager had spent some time with his

own people trying to analyze what they were doing that might cause trouble for manufacturing. Making too many design changes late in the game, specifying 'unobtanium' for the parts, not asking questions about producibility, things like that.

Now I have really begged the question. There was something fundamentally different in the two project teams that I haven't yet mentioned. The second team – the 'effective' one – had undergone some purposive education within itself on this matter of how to function more effectively on an interpersonal level.

To be more specific, the second project group had delved deeply into a self-evaluative process known as 'team building', while the first group had not but was operating pretty much on its own instincts and common sense.

As I describe team building, it's important to keep in mind that it's part of an emerging 'managerial technology' called Organization Development. There are several streams making up the main body of this rather fluid field. One came out of sensitivity training, which I'll compare with team building shortly. Another stream in organization development includes things like job design, job enlargement and enrichment, career development and so on.

Team building has its place in a developing human-systems approach to organizations. This means that it should not be thought of as a gimmick, a one-shot technique that will solve all your problems. Lots of companies have gone at it that way and have failed miserably. If used at all, it should be used with a full awareness that it's a continuing thing and that there are other, related techniques which ought to be considered along with it.

As I use it, the 'team' in team building refers to any organizational element whose members have a common supervisor. They are also a team in the sense that they have some common task or tasks to perform.

Now the 'building' part of team building refers to the notion that the members of the group will spend some time together where their agenda is 'how might we improve our effectiveness as a team?' . . . where they step back from actually doing the job and take a look at it in a behavioral sense. Things like how they're organized; how they make decisions, how they resolve conflicts; the quality of their staff meetings; interpersonal problems that might exist; issues they have with other teams; hidden agendas (for example, you go into a meeting ostensibly to discuss the design of a new control system, but your real goal is to knife those so-and-so circuit designers) and so on.

Early in an organization's attempt to use this 'technology' it is critical to use an outside consultant or, if such exists, an inside consultant to facilitate the process. In either case you need someone with some training in the behavioral sciences and, more importantly, practise in the application of team building as a part of organization development.

You need significant blocks of time to deal with the kinds of issues that come up in team building. It's not something that you can do in an hour, or two hours, or three hours. Getting started may take a couple of days of uninterrupted time. And the whole team has to be involved, by definition. If this requirement simply can't be met in your organization, don't even think about getting involved in team building.

We don't seem to have the time to be taught very much about collaborating with others. But we need this ability because we're so dependent on others: to get that piece of hardware built, you and I have to work together effectively right across our disciplines. For psychological and social reasons that sometimes go right back into childhood, we tend to make a situation that could be collaborative into one that is competitive – where much of our energy is spent trying to have one of us win and the other lose, rather than focusing it all on getting on with the job.

Now team building won't resolve all such human issues in the culture of the group that attempts it; that's a very unrealistic expectation. But the evidence is that the technique can lead to small improvements in the kinds of issues that I mentioned earlier and – most important – these improvements have an enormous leverage in bettering the effectiveness of the group as a whole.

For example, overriding all the issues I described earlier is the issue of trust. In my experience with team building, I have seen that if the trust level in a group is improved by, say, 5 per cent, the performance level of the group seems to rise a lot more. It doesn't mean that people become completely trusting of one another, but that there's increased trust, and that has a great impact on things. Less games are being played. For example, I don't waste energy in meetings any more with a hidden agenda of trying to be sure you don't take over my domain; rather, the energy goes into getting the project on the track. Enormous amounts of energy can be expended in meetings by kicking around this sort of interpersonal debris.

There are five different situations in organizations where team building can be useful:

One place where team building can be used is with a new team: a new engineering project is starting, or a new staff group is being formed, or a new laboratory is to be set up, or a new division in the company, or a new plant location.

The second kind of team-building situation is akin to the first – a new team is forming, but some of the people in it are from other companies or organizations. This is quite common in the aero-space industry, where a number of contractors, sub-contractors, government monitors, and so on are combined. It happens, too, in other industries or businesses, in government, in universities, in labor unions.

The team that has existed for some time is the third team-building situation I want to mention. I'll come back to it when we look at the actual mechanics of the process, for it's typically the kind that's done when an organization first attempts to apply the technique.

The fourth team building situation is where the team has existed for some time but feels that it is in trouble. In this case, the team building obviously ought to focus on the problems, at least initially, as they are identified by the people in the group.

This group is in the process of moving into the last category of team building I want to touch on – the team that has existed for some time and has, on several occasions, done team building as I'm describing it in this article.

This is an important category to keep in mind, because I want to emphasize in all of this a sense of continuity – not one-shot magic that fixes everything up forever. Human beings in work groups will always have issues to deal with. The issues will vary over the course of time. Team building is simply a way of dealing rationally with those issues as they come up, and of making significant improvements on some of them.

Now that we've looked at the 'why' and the 'where' of team building, we're about ready for the 'how'. First, though, I want to answer a question that comes up all the time: 'What you're talking about sounds an awful lot like sensitivity training; is team building something different?' Yes, it is different from sensitivity training – or T-groups, or encounter groups, or grid labs, or any of the other names that are used for that sort of thing. Let me explain this.

Sensitivity training typically involves a group of people who are strangers to one another, or who are at most 'cousins' – people in the same organization, but in different parts of it. That is one way it differs: it doesn't involve a group of people who are in a team having a common supervisor.

The other difference is that there is really a different agenda. In sensitivity training, the agenda is really my learning – as an individual – some things about myself, about myself in groups, about groups themselves, about work cultures and related subjects. It's quite literally a training session, with a definite beginning and ending, while team building is on-the-job introspection among a group of people who work together more or less continuously.

Now the theory base and the way the 'leader' of each kind of session goes at things aren't all that different. It's just that the relationship between the people involved and their agendas are different. You certainly don't have to do sensitivity training as a prerequisite to team building. It could be very helpful if you do, but it isn't necessary.

At this point I want to get down to the 'how' of team building, in a way that you can perceive the essential ingredients and steps.

A key ingredient is the third-party consultant I mentioned earlier. I use the phrase 'third-party' to suggest that this man is an outsider in the sense that he is not caught up in the particular work culture being worked on. That doesn't mean he can be objective about the team he's working with, but that he can relate to it differently, and see issues and help raise things that other people can't see because they're too close to it. In effect, he doesn't have at stake what all the others have.

The first time around, I think it's wise to have as the third party someone from outside the organization – a consultant with some background in behavioral science and practice in team building. You might have such a man in personnel, and, if so, use him. As your experience grows you will develop your own skilled third parties elsewhere within the organization. We've found at TRW Systems, for example, that engineers or engineering managers who have interest and experience in team building, and some exposure to sensitivity training, make excellent 'consultants' for us.

Now let's see how the consultant works with the team. First of all, the team members should know who he is and have a pretty good understanding of what his role is going to be, before the team building begins.

Once the consultant and the team manager have gotten to know each other somewhat, the rest of the preparatory process isn't very elaborate. The team manager simply calls a staff meeting, introduces Mr X as someone who is going to work with the team, and says something like this: 'I'd like to do some team building, and our agenda is going to be "how can we improve our effectiveness?" I think there are some issues we need to deal with, including my own behavior as a leader, so let's try this out.' This is then followed by some discussion of what's going to happen.

The next step – perhaps at the close of the staff meeting – would be to have a significant block of time set aside when the consultant can get together with the group and explore the question 'How can we improve our effectiveness as a team?' The block of time can vary considerably, but typically it's a couple of days for a first effort in team building. Let's say two to three days for a team of, say, eight to sixteen people.

Just prior to this large block of time, maybe a day or two before but not much more than that, the consultant will interview each member of the team for a half-hour or an hour. The usual ground-rule is that the data the third-party consultant collects is public data. That is, everyone understands that when the group meeting begins, he is going to feed back what he thought he heard in the interviews – the kinds of problems the individual team members identified, were concerned about, and would like to see discussed.

The interviews have several purposes. One is to give the consultant a current feel for what is going on. The interviews also enable him to throw that first impression quickly into the group, by providing a reading of the system by someone who is pretty sensitive and can understand fairly well what people are saying. The interviews also start people doing their homework: they know they're going to talk with the consultant first; they've met him already; they know there's going to be this block of time for discussion; and the interview process helps them to sort out the issues they think are most important.

You are probably wondering whether the issues the team members raise in the interviews are fed back to the group in a 'personalized' way, or in a 'generalized' way. It can be done either way. The important thing is that whatever is done with the data is understood in advance. You don't want to have everyone wondering, 'Can we trust the consultant?' because that would just be a diverting issue.

I have come to prefer personalizing the feedback – being specific about identifying who raised what issue, except on those few points where the man being interviewed doesn't want to be identified. People are really quite candid and want to discuss important issues openly. Besides, it's pretty hard to camouflage your own concern about a given issue in a discussion, so why not identify yourself with it from the outset? However, if your team prefers to have the feedback generalized on the first time around, by all means do it that way. The important thing is to start to deal with meaningful issues, to get the process underway.

Once the interviews are completed, the two to three day block of time can begin. Quite often this takes place somewhere else in the plant, the laboratory, or the office building where the team does its work. Or it can be in a near-by motel. The important thing is that a location be picked where you won't be interrupted by phones and where you can be as informal as possible. If they want to, people should be able to take off their ties, put their feet up, and not have a lot of furniture between them. Having as little between the team members as possible physically helps a great deal psychologically in dealing with these human issues.

At the beginning of the period of time, the head of the team should remind people why they're here: 'The agenda is to improve our effectiveness as a team. We've had these interviews, and now let's talk as frankly as we can. Anything is up for grabs, including my own functioning in the group. Let's begin with our consultant telling us what he heard in his interviews.'

At this point the consultant spends about ten or twenty minutes feeding back briefly the themes, the main issues, the sense of the team that he picked up during the interview process – in the language and with the flavor of the people he interviewed. He doesn't feed back everything, not because he's hiding anything, but because it would take too much time. Nor does he propose solutions. That would be premature, and the solutions ought to emerge out of the group anyway.

Usually, but not always, the feedback process starts with issues relating to the top man on the team. There are inevitably things he is doing that need discussing – few leaders are perfect – and if he's not going to go along with the team-building process, the rest of the team isn't either. The third-party consultant interviewed him in the preparatory stage, tried to listen hard for issues involving him, and now uses his willingness to learn how his men feel about his leadership as a lever to get the discussion going more broadly. That's why the leader has to want to do team building, and have good rapport with the consultant from the beginning.

What sort of issues might relate to the top man? Well, they can be relatively mechanical ones like: how frequently does he see individuals on the team? How often does he have staff meetings?

Are they long enough? Too long? Or, there can be issues relating to the decision-making process that the leader uses: do people feel involved? Do they feel they have a chance to influence decisions? Or do they feel he is constantly deciding important things without really involving or consulting with his people?

There can be issues with respect to how he handles conflicts. Some heads of groups don't like to see conflicts discussed. If two people in the group start arguing, he reacts almost like a parent saying, in effect, 'now children, don't fight; we're all one happy family, so let's get on with it.' The trouble with that, of course, is that it doesn't resolve the conflict, it just submerges it.

As often happens, of course, the dispute may involve the leader himself. In such a conflict, he may be the type of leader who never loses and always wins. Not because he's always right, but because in the end he uses his power, and the argument goes his way regardless of the facts.

With issues like this explored out in the open, the process can move on to issues among peers in the group.

There can, for example, be issues of trust that exist among the team members. Maybe someone feels that someone else is spending a lot of his energy trying to look right so he can get the promotion when the time comes. His drawer is full of 'Pearl Harbor files', memos that document everything the group decides to do, but show him in a favorable light in case anything goes wrong.

Or perhaps someone is very self-centered about his own technical specialty. To him, if he is an antenna man, the project looks like an antenna, and he isn't willing to look at the tradeoffs involved. He couldn't care less about the other sub-systems and how they interact with his. So in a functional and even personal sense he is behaving selfishly, and that could be an issue.

There can be issues between people regarding their styles of operating with one another. Some people, for example, are so aggressive in making a point that they turn other people off. How many times have you said to yourself in a meeting, 'Well here comes Charlie again, and the first ten minutes are going to be thunder and lightning, and then he'll get to his point'? By the time he does, of course, you're so annoyed you don't even listen to his point, which might be a damn good one. All those verbal atmospherics and their consequence are clearly a waste of energy, and ought to be discussed.

In teams that have existed for a while, there can be unresolved personal issues like these that have been festering for a long time. Someone hasn't trusted a colleague for several years, starting with a particular incident, and then the mistrust accelerated because we all deal with each other partially through stereotypes – a set of assumptions about each other that go untested because we never talk about them.

Now in my experience, when people who aren't trusting each other sit down in a team-building session and talk about it, they move toward each other. They move beyond that mistrust and really get to the issues that are involved. I'm not saying that in team building you can go from a lot of mistrust to complete trust. But you can move from a lot of mistrust to less of it and some trust, and that shift has an enormous leverage effect on the group's effectiveness.

What the third-party consultant is trying to do, in a gross sense, is to get these issues that have almost been discussed, that people have been on the edge of talking about, out on the table and faced squarely.

There are several things that the consultant is trying to facilitate in the process. One is getting the team members to really hear each other and to understand the issues in a relatively nondefensive way. He tries to prepare the top man to be nondefensive, and lets him set the example.

Suppose staff meetings are an issue in the group, and the consultant is sure that, in discussing that issue someone is bound to say, 'I don't like the way you conduct staff meetings.' The consultant points out to the top man that the inappropriate response would be to say, 'That's too bad; that's the way I conduct them and I'm the boss.' He suggests that the more appropriate response might be, 'All right, go on, what don't you like about them? I'd really like to understand what you don't like and to suspend judgement for the moment.' So when the team members see the top man really listen, and not get defensive, some of them will too, and the process is on its way.

The consultant may have to intervene if someone in the group is getting overly defensive. But experience shows that people get to enjoy hearing each other, and will assume the consultant's role to keep the discussion focused on an issue.

The second thing the consultant strives for is a realization on the part of the team members that there are alternatives to the present ways of functioning. In most instances this doesn't prove too difficult to do, because experience with team building shows that after people really hear each other they get more optimistic and creative, and they search quite widely for alternative modes of behavior.

Take a man who is overly aggressive in discussing project matters with his colleagues. In the team-building session, one of his co-workers may say 'Look, I really run away from you. I don't want to get in an argument with you because you win every time, and there's no point in it. I've never been able to convince you that I have a point.' Now if he has begun to listen like the others in the group, and if he isn't totally arrogant, that comment is bound to concern him. He'll begin to think about other ways of responding to his colleagues. He won't alter his behavior completely; that's too much to expect. But he'll become somewhat easier to deal with – and that's a plus.

If the third-party consultant and the group have been working well together, there's a third major phenomenon that quite often takes place. After some productive work on their own interpersonal issues, quite often the team members will explore their relationships with other groups in the organization with whom they have to interact.

After a while, perhaps with the consultant's prodding, they will begin to ask themselves a very important introspective question, one that represents great behavioral progress: 'Are we a part of the problem we're talking about?' The moment that question is asked, a very different game begins to get played, for in every case you'll find there are things the team is doing that contribute to intergroup problems.

It may well be that there are issues that can't be dealt with in team-building terms. Perhaps there really is incompetence in another group; maybe manufacturing really cannot deliver on schedule because of other commitments. But usually there are also issues in the relationships – group to group – that the team is contributing to and hasn't dealt with very constructively until now.

Suppose, during their early discussion of other groups in the organization, the team zeros in on manufacturing. They may feel that there is chaos down on the factory floor: if you ask them where part so-and-so is, they don't know; if you ask when such-and-such part will be built, they give you a glassy stare, because they're not sure; sub-assemblies aren't being delivered on time, and nobody seems to know why; and so on. Pretty soon, after some helling and damning about those black-hats down in manufacturing, maybe someone will say, 'You know, we've received a bunch of contract changes on that project recently, and maybe we're switching priorities on those guys too often. Maybe we should send someone down to find out whether that is contributing to their problems.' And with this suggestion, the group has made a big step forward in the team-building process.

To avoid having the block of time be simply a bull session, where everyone winds up feeling good and warm about it all, but where little change occurs on the job, the top man should make a determined effort to develop written action items. Toward the end there should be a summing up: 'Let's understand who is going to do what and when.' Typically, the group might come up with ten or fifteen such action items, and they might range quite widely. Some will be quite mechanical: let's have a staff meeting once a week instead of once a month; and some of that time ought to be blocked off for more process work – looking at how we function. There may be an issue within the group that needs more work. Perhaps three people have a problem among themselves, have started to deal with it in the session just ending, but haven't quite finished. An action item might be for them to get together on their own and work on it, with or without consulting help.

131

Issues between the team and other groups in the organization will have to be dealt with – such as the manufacturing problem I cited a moment ago. There, the action item is to send someone to assess the impact of the project team on this functional group.

But suppose there was a trust issue between two heads of sub-units. The two managers may have come closer together psychologically during the team-building period, but if there was mistrust between them at the outset, that mistrust is magnified down below. In coming to trust each other a bit more, they've created greater psychological distance between themselves and those who work for them, so an action item would be to figure out a way to deal with that.

With its list of action items complete, the group is just about ready to adjourn its team-building session. The remaining thing to be done is to hold a brief critique of the proceedings – to try and be explicit about what we think we learned from all of this.

This is important to do, because one of the vital questions before the house is: can we learn to deal in a more sophisticated, mature and efficient way with our human issues? Or, to put it a bit differently: can we start a learning curve here which gets us much more equipped to cope with these issues?

Now let me step back from all of this and quickly sum up what I've been trying to say about team building and its broader context:

In advanced technology organizations, the nature of the work forces us to work in interdisciplinary teams. The effective functioning of teams is therefore an important management issue.

The second point is that when we say, 'business is business; let's keep personalities out of it,' we're talking nonsense. Management doesn't have the choice of not dealing with interpersonal relationships; the question is how do you deal with them?

My third point is that since we have to work together across our technical disciplines, we'd better learn how to work collaboratively rather than competitively. We have beautiful ways of cancelling each other out: not hearing, not building, putting down our colleagues, etc., rather than somehow seeing how we can use our talents together.

Fourth, I want to stress that in trying to deal with issues like this there has to be a sense of continuity. People resist change and cultures certainly resist change. This is not a weakness in human nature, it's simply a fact. Don't look at team building as a quick fix, because it isn't.

Some other books published by Penguin
are described on the following pages.

THE SOCIAL PSYCHOLOGY OF WORK

Michael Argyle

In this survey of social behavior at work and of the social factors that affect our experience of employment, Michael Argyle traces the biological and historical origins of work and contrasts various contemporary forms of work organization, including those in Japan, Israel, and Yugoslavia. Among much else, this book looks at the roles of status, technology, working groups, personality, social organization, incentives, leadership, and other social skills and at the effects of these variables on productivity, job satisfaction, labor turnover, and absenteeism. Michael Argyle is on the faculty of Oxford University.

MANAGEMENT OF CHANGE AND CONFLICT

Edited by John M. Thomas and Warren G. Bennis

This collection of essays on the management of change in organizations recognizes the interdependence of planned change and conflict. The editors have grouped their selections under six headings, which include "The Future Context of Organizational Change and Conflict," "Issues and Concepts in Organizational Change and Innovation," "The Practice of Planned Organizational Change," and "The Management of Conflict." Among the eighteen individual articles are S. Terreberry's "The Evolution of Organizational Environments," W. F. Whyte's "Models for Building and Changing Organizations," M. Deutsch's "Productive and Destructive Conflict," and W. Gamson's "The Management of Discontent." John M. Thomas and Warren G. Bennis are respectively Acting Director of the University and Vice-President of Academic Development, State University of New York at Buffalo.